All About
SHORT
SELLING

THE EASY WAY TO GET STARTED

OTHER TITLES IN THE "ALL ABOUT" FINANCE SERIES

All About
SHORT
SELLING

THE EASY WAY TO GET STARTED

TOM TAULLI

New York   Chicago   San Francisco   Lisbon   London   Madrid
Mexico City   Milan   New Delhi   San Juan   Seoul
Singapore   Sydney   Toronto

The **McGraw·Hill** Companies

1 2 3 4 5 6 7 8 9 0   DOC/DOC   1 9 8 7 6 5 4 3 2 1

ISBN: 978-0-07-175934-2
MHID: 0-07-175934-4

This publication is designed to provide accurate and authoritative information in regard to the subject matter covered. It is sold with the understanding that neither the author nor the publisher is engaged in rendering legal, accounting, or other professional service. If legal advice or other expert assistance is required, the services of a competent professional person should be sought.
—*From a Declaration of Principles Jointly Adopted by
a Committee of the American Bar Association and
a Committee of Publishers and Associations*

Library of Congress Cataloging-in-Publication Data

Taulli, Tom, 1968–
  All about short selling / by Tom Taulli.
      p. cm.
  Includes bibliographical references and index.
  ISBN 978-0-07-175934-2 (alk. paper)
  1. Short selling. 2. Speculation. I. Title.
  HG6041.T378 2011
  332.63'2283—dc22

McGraw-Hill books are available at special quantity discounts to use as premiums and sales promotions, or for use in corporate training programs. To contact a representative, please visit the Contact Us pages at www.mhprofessional.com.

This book is printed on acid-free paper.

CONTENTS

Chapter 11

Chapter 12

Chapter 13

Chapter 14

Chapter 15

Chapter 16

All About
SHORT
SELLING

THE EASY WAY TO GET STARTED

CHAPTER 1

What Is Short Selling and How Can It Help Your Investing?

Key Concepts

- Reasons for short selling
- What is short selling?
- How to short
- The history of short selling

One of the key tenets for money managers is to focus on investing for the long term. Over the years, the volatile swings will even out and your portfolio will steadily increase. By taking a buy-and-hold strategy, you should be able to generate 7 percent to 8 percent average returns—when including dividends. This is what history tends to show.

But is this really true? Can the markets be stagnant for ten or even twenty years? Yes they can. Keep in mind that the time between 2000 to 2010 is often referred to as the "Lost Decade," in which the Standard & Poor's 500 Index (S&P 500) averaged a loss of 0.5 percent per year (of course, it would have been even worse when adjusted for inflation). This did not even happen during the 1930s when the United States suffered from the Great Depression.

It is true that statistics can be misleading, as the first half of 2000 was the peak of the bull market. If the comparison was done from 2002, the numbers would look better. Yet few would argue that 2000 to 2010 was not without extreme volatility. In all, there were two major declines in the markets, which included 2000 to 2002 and 2007 to 2008. The decade also saw a variety of negative events. There was the real estate implosion, the accounting scandals of Enron and WorldCom, the terrorist strike on 9/11, the wars in Iraq and Afghanistan, and two recessions.

But can there be two lost decades? Looking back at U.S. history, there are examples of this. For example, the 1929 crash led to a grueling bear market. The Dow Jones Industrial Average (DJIA) did not recover until 1954. Another case is the period from 1964 to 1982, which also saw a devastating bear market. There is also the terrible experience in Japan. Since the plunge in the Nikkei Index in 1989, the markets are still 75 percent off from the peak.

Unfortunately, the U.S. economy is certainly facing major headwinds, which could make it difficult for the markets to post strong gains. Consider the views of top money managers at Pimco like Tony Crescenzi, Mohamed El-Erian, and Bill Gross. They believe that the U.S. economy will have a muted growth path for the long haul. One reason is that many of the jobs lost in the 2008–2009 recession will no longer return. Industries like autos, housing, construction, retail, and finance have undergone tremendous structural changes. Corporate America has also learned how to manage with fewer employees by using productivity-enhancing technologies and outsourcing to economies like China and India.

There has also been a massive destruction of wealth. Since peaking at $66 trillion, the overall net worth of Americans has fallen by about $10 trillion. This will likely be a drag on consumer spending, especially as the Baby Boomers get older and start to retire. They will focus on more conservative investments because they do not want to run out of capital. Another major drag on the economy will be increased regulations. True, the near collapse of the financial system meant that it was inevitable that the federal government would get much more intrusive. Yet this will make it more difficult for companies to operate. Despite the regulations, it is likely that U.S. financial institutions will be restrained in extending credit. The fact is the consumers still have large debt loads. What's more, with lower growth prospects, there is not as much need for credit.

The costs of the bailouts will also lead to higher taxes. At some point, the federal government will need to take action to reduce the swelling budget deficit. And in light of the surge of retirements from the Baby Boomers—which will mean higher healthcare and Social Security benefits—it will be tough to find ways to cut costs.

In light of the potential challenges—and the complexities of global economies—investors are likely to face more risk and volatility in the future. This is not to say investors need to avoid stocks or put money into ultra-safe securities like U.S. Treasuries. Instead, it means that it is important to look beyond just the purchase of securities—and consider how to make money when the values of investments fall. And of course, one effective way to do this is to use the investment technique of short selling.

MORE BAD STOCKS THAN GOOD ONES?

While any investor can have a hot streak, it typically does not last. Only a handful of investors have been able to consistently beat the markets over a ten-year period, such as Warren Buffett and Peter Lynch. Even with those who have achieved this feat—like Bill Miller—there is often a period when the returns eventually fall off.

The key to getting above-market returns is to find a few stellar performers. Picking stocks like Starbucks or Microsoft in their early years would have more than offset the losers and average performers. Lynch famously called these investments "ten baggers" (since they increased ten times or more).

Consider Li Lu, who is a candidate to manage Buffett's $100 billion portfolio. Since 1998, his hedge fund has posted annualized compound returns of 26.4 percent. This compares to the Standard & Poor's return of 2.25 percent. However, a large part of the success came from an investment in BYD, which is a fast-growing Chinese battery maker.[1] Needless to say, it is exceedingly difficult to find these home runs. In fact, Li has found only one in his career. Actually, the fact is that—even for top investors—the chances are higher that a typical stock pick will fall in value. In other words, the odds tend to be in favor of short sellers.

---

[1] http://online.wsj.com/article/SB10001424052748703977004575393180048272028 .html?dbk.

This appears to be the case from a study by Blackstar Funds. The investment firm looked at the performance of all U.S. stocks from 1983 to 2006. Given that this was during a large bull market, the typical return should have been strong, right? The conclusion is the opposite. About 39 percent of the stocks were unprofitable and 18.5 percent lost at least 75 percent of their value. Only a quarter of the stocks accounted for all the value of the market.[2]

REASONS FOR SHORT SELLING

Until recently, the topic of short selling was fairly obscure. It mostly made headline news when there was a major drop in the markets. As should be no surprise, the short sellers are easy targets to blame when things go wrong. Because of this, there are lots of misconceptions about short selling. In many investment books, the topic is rarely mentioned. And if it is, the coverage is spotty. Yet after the 2007–2008 financial panic, short selling has increasingly become a part of the investor's vernacular. As a sign of this, it has become a daily topic on CNBC as well as in top publications like the *Wall Street Journal* and *Barron's*. In fact, one of CNBC's top journalists, Herb Greenberg, often covers short-sale targets.

So even if you do not short sell a stock, it is still important to understand the conversation. You may not even realize that some of your investments may actually employ short-selling approaches. Or, by using the analytical techniques of a short seller, you may be able to avoid stocks that are vulnerable for a big fall. But if you do short sell—or want to do so—there are certainly important benefits. Perhaps one of the biggest is that short selling can lower the overall risk in your portfolio. If 80 or 90 percent of your portfolio has long positions, then a fall in the market will be partially offset by your short positions. This would have certainly been a big help to many investors during the 2007–2008 financial panic. Keep in mind, too, that some of the world's top investors, such as hedge fund managers, routinely use short selling because it can hedge the downside in a portfolio. Examples include George Soros and Julian Robertson, who are billionaires.

---

[2] http://www.blackstarfunds.com/files/TheCapitalismDistribution.pdf.

Short selling can also result in quick returns. It is often the case that a stock will fall faster and farther than when a stock increases. A reason for this is that investors may panic when there is bad news and dump large amounts of shares. When this happens, it can be tough to find buyers.

It is actually getting easier to short sell securities. Over the years, Wall Street has introduced a variety of new innovations like exchange-traded funds (ETFs). These allow investors to make money when stock indexes fall. It is also possible to short real estate, commodities, and even countries. Despite these advantages, investors are often reluctant to engage in short selling. The perceived risks are high and the process can be somewhat confusing. Interestingly enough, some investors think it is even un-American to short sell stocks. Consider that some thought the short sellers were the cause of the financial shock of 2008. Regardless, the fact remains that short selling is common in any modern market and attempts to make it illegal have often failed.

WHAT IS SHORT SELLING?

Short selling is pervasive throughout the world's stock markets. To get a sense of the activity, look at the short interest activity on the New York Stock Exchange (NYSE) in mid-June of 2010. The volume was 18 billion shares, which represented about 4.75 percent of the stock outstanding. Yet even though short selling is a big part of the markets, the fact is that many investors still have only a vague idea of how the process works. Perhaps the main reason is that it sounds counterintuitive. How is it possible to make money when a stock's value falls? This is actually possible because short selling *reverses* the process that people buy stock. That is, you sell the stock first and then you sell it later—hopefully at a lower price. If so, you will make a profit on the trade.

Let's look at this in more detail. First of all, an investor must find shares that can be borrowed. This is known as "the locate" or "the borrow." Just about any brokerage firm has a department that focuses on this type of security. Keep in mind that it can be difficult, if not impossible, to borrow shares. This may be the case if the stock is already heavily shorted and the brokerage firms are hesitant to engage in the trade. Or, it could be that a stock is lightly traded and there are few shares available to short. Because of this, an investor may look at alternatives. One approach is to purchase a "put option." This is a security that increases in value when the underlying security falls. Or, an investor may short a futures contract on an index or even stocks.

These approaches can result in quick profits because of the leverage. That is, an investor need only put up 5 percent to 50 percent of the overall value of the contract. But, of course, if the trade does not work, the losses can be substantial.

Let's assume you can borrow shares in XYZ Corp., which you believe will fall in value over the next couple of months. To do this, you must first set up a margin account and have sufficient assets in your account. This is often $5,000 or more. You then borrow 100 shares of XYZ Corp., which have a price of $40. You will then sell the shares and generate proceeds of $4,000. The process is often done within minutes or even seconds. The proceeds from this transaction will then be kept in the account as security. Suppose a few months pass by and the shares of XYZ Corp. fall to $30. You can take your profit by "covering" your short. This means you will buy 100 shares for $30 and return them to your brokerage firm. In the end, you will have generated a $1,000 profit ($4,000 minus $3,000).

THE CONTROVERSIAL HISTORY OF SHORT SELLING

Short selling is far from new. It got its start when stock exchanges emerged in Europe in the late 1500s. One of the hottest markets was in Amsterdam, which saw a massive bull market. A top firm during those heady times was the East Indies Company. Even with all the excitement and bullishness, there were some investors who were skeptical, such as Isaac Le Maire. A top merchant, he had a good sense of the value of a company as well as how to detect troubles.

Based on his research, Le Maire believed that the East Indies Company was poised for a big fall. So he aggressively shorted the stock and even spread negative rumors about the company. He was ultimately proved correct in 1610 when the shares of the East Indies Company collapsed. The event was so significant that the bull market ended. Looking for a reason, investors pointed to Le

Maire and other short sellers. The upshot was that the Dutch government banned short selling. But this turned out to be useless as investors found creative ways to get around the rules.

This would not be the end of the controversy or the banning of short selling. The U.S. markets have also seen a variety of fights. The first ban came in 1812 when the country was embroiled in a tough war. But over time, investors found loopholes. It helped that the New York Stock Exchange was fairly inactive, with just a few dozen companies traded on the market. So by the late 1850s, the United States ended the short-selling ban.

After the Civil War, the markets in the United States boomed as the country became industrialized. Railroads raised large amounts of capital from Wall Street, as did other industrial companies. There were also new innovations, like the telegraph and the ticker tape. Increasingly, the United States was becoming an economic superpower. And, stock market trading was getting much more sophisticated. With few regulations, a variety of entrepreneurs—known as "Robber Barons"—amassed huge fortunes. Unfortunately, it was not uncommon for them to engage in market manipulation, false rumors, and even bribery. It certainly was a Darwinian environment.

An example was Daniel Drew. Despite being illiterate, he had an innate sense for making large sums of money. He eventually teamed up with Jay Gould and Jim Fisk. Over time, they would speculate on the stock market—in terms of buying stock and selling short. Their only goal was to make as much money as possible.

It should be no surprise that corporate executives would also participate in questionable activities. Consider John Gates, who was the president of American Steel and Wire Company. When he realized business was softening, he cut back production and laid off employees. At the same time, he shorted his company's stock and made a tidy profit.

Even with several major market crashes and depressions, the U.S. government did nothing to restrain short selling. One reason was the belief in free markets. Shouldn't investors be allowed to make money—even if the markets fall? But this attitude would change as the stock market crashed in 1929 and the economy sunk into the Great Depression. By 1933, the Dow Jones Industrial Average fell by a staggering 89 percent.

During these tough times, some traders actually did make a fortune by short selling. One was Jesse Livermore. He had a photographic memory for stock movements. In fact, because of this, he was able to see patterns in stock changes, which ultimately became the basis of "technical analysis." It was during 1929 that Livermore made his biggest trade. He made roughly $100 million by shorting the stock market. Yet it was somewhat of a Pyrrhic victory. The American public believed he was the cause of the crash and even the terrible economic problems. As a result, Livermore hired bodyguards and eventually committed suicide in 1940.

Besides Livermore, another great Wall Street trader made a fortune from the 1929 crash: Bernard Baruch. He actually wrote a book on the topic called *Short Sales and the Manipulation of Securities*. It was an attempt to show that short selling was not harmful. For example, he demonstrated that the concept is prevalent in many industries. After all, don't many farmers sell their crops before they plant anything? Or home builders sell homes before they are made?

Despite this defense of short selling, Baruch showed little progress in making his case. Instead, he tried to keep a low profile of his trading activities, which was definitely a good idea. Keep in mind that he would eventually become a top adviser to presidents Harding, Coolidge, and Hoover. In the aftermath of the stock market crash, Congress and President Roosevelt brought about substantial federal regulations of securities and created the Securities and Exchange Commission (SEC). What's more, the federal government imposed various regulations on short selling, including the "uptick rule" (which means it is not legal to short a stock when the price is falling) and margin requirements so as to reduce the risks and volatility. But these reforms did little to stop short selling.

Actually, by the 1950s, the emergence of hedge funds would make short selling a common practice on Wall Street. With volatile markets, these hedge fund managers skillfully shorted the market. Interestingly enough, they would target brand name companies like Coca-Cola, GE, and McDonald's.

Then by the 1980s, there was yet another important development in the evolution of short selling: short-only funds. The innovators were three brothers—Matt, Kurt, and Joe Feshbach. All they did was find short-sale opportunities—and they were certainly skilled at it. Then again, they engaged in a tremendous amount of research.

In some cases, the Feshbach brothers would uncover frauds. This was the situation with ZZZZ Best Company, which quickly went bust and generated a considerable profit for the brothers. With such successes, the Feshbach brothers were able to raise a $1 billion fund. But as the bull market resumed in the 1990s, the returns trailed off and the fund eventually changed its mandate to include long positions.

Another top short-only fund to come out during the 1980s was Kynikos Associates, led by Jim Chanos. He is considered one of the best short sellers of his generation. Keep in mind that he spotted such trades as Enron and Boston Market.

THE BENEFITS OF SHORT SELLING

Despite the rancor about the evils of short selling, the fact is that there are many benefits to the practice. If anything, it is essential for the functioning of a modern marketplace. Consider when the U.S. government placed a ban on short selling during late 2008; it was actually limited to roughly 800 financial stocks. At the same time, there were a variety of exceptions, such as for market makers who needed to facilitate trades for buyers and sellers. In other words, short selling is critical for providing liquidity to the marketplace. As Bernard Baruch once said, "To enjoy the advantages of a free market, one must have both buyers and sellers, both bulls and bears. A market without bears would be like a nation without a free press. There would be no one to criticize and restrain the false optimism that always leads to disaster."

Short selling can also help to dampen asset bubbles. In fact, if it was easier to short sell real estate, the impact of the real estate bubble may have been less severe. Although, some savvy investors, like John Paulson, were able to use sophisticated financial instruments—called derivatives—to essentially short the subprime real estate mortgage market. By doing this, Paulson generated billions in profits. Interestingly enough, some short sellers, like David Einhorn and William Ackman, uncovered companies committing fraud. Examples included Boston Chicken, Crazy Eddie, Sunbeam, and Enron.

What's more, short selling allows for "hedging" of a portfolio, which protects the gains when the market falls, and it is also an effective way to employ advanced investing strategies. One approach is "arbitrage." This is a way to make a profit when the same security or similar ones have different valuations. These trades are often quick and require sophisticated computer systems.

NAKED SHORT SELLING

Although there are certainly many benefits to short selling, this does not mean it is without its problems. As with any large market, there are investors who engage in questionable or even illegal activities. This is the case with "naked short selling" (also known as a "fail to deliver" trade), when an investor shorts a stock without borrowing the underlying shares. An investor may do this because of difficulties in finding shares to borrow. Or, the cost of a short sale may be prohibitive. However, in U.S. stock exchanges—as well as many other foreign stock exchanges—naked short selling is illegal. This is according to SEC Regulation SHO. Why is this so? The belief is that naked short selling could potentially allow for an unlimited short position, which could ultimately drive down the stock. Actually, this was one of the complaints during the 2007–2008 financial panic.

Despite this, there is still much controversy. That is, various companies and traders believe that naked short selling is fairly common but the laws are rarely enforced. In fact, a sudden rise in failed-to-deliver trades may indicate that a stock is experiencing heavy levels of naked short selling. For example, Regulation SHO provides for a "Threshold Security List," which shows a stock where more than 0.5 percent of the outstanding shares have failed to deliver for five business days. Ironically enough, short sellers consider this a guide for companies that may be good short trades.

The controversies are likely to continue, as they have throughout history. But the fact remains that short selling continues to be an effective investment tool. As seen in this chapter, it helps with not only getting strong gains but hedging a portfolio. In the next chapter, we will take a look at the essentials of short selling, such as margin accounts and tax issues.

CHAPTER 2

Characteristics
of Short Selling

Key Concepts

- Cash and margin accounts
- Capital gains and losses
- Worthless securities
- Short-selling deductions
- Shorting against the box

Since short selling is a specialized area, it is a good idea to spend time selecting a brokerage firm. You can check Google and use a firm's name with the phrase "short selling." This should be a good start in your search. As you narrow down the firms, you can also look at brokerage surveys, such as from *Barron's* or *Smart Money*. Something else that is useful is to check out a firm's regulatory history at FINRA Brokercheck (www.finra.org/Brokercheck or 800-289-9999).

To get started with short selling, you will need to set up a cash account and a margin account. While there are a variety of details for this process, it is not necessarily tough. But it is important to not rush. Of course, if you have any questions, ask the brokerage firm. Make sure you ask for a margin specialist, who is likely to understand the many nuances of short selling. Finally, taxes can be a big

factor in short selling in terms of your ultimate return on investment (ROI). There are a variety of rules that restrict the tax advantages and potential deductions for your trading.

CASH ACCOUNT

The cash account is the most basic brokerage account and it is the
first one you must establish before you can sell short. The setup
process is fairly easy and the form is only a couple of pages long.
On it, you will provide details like your Social Security number,
employment history, investment experience and objectives, annual
income, and net worth. These questions seem intrusive but the brokerage firm has no choice. They are required to meet many regulations; one of the most important is called "Know Thy Client."

Of course, the brokerage firm will need to notify the Internal
Revenue Service (IRS) and local tax authorities. There are even
requirements to guard against potential terrorist threats, such as
with the U.S. Patriot Act. Because of all this, make sure the information you provide is accurate. This is important, especially if you
wind up in a dispute with your brokerage firm. Accordingly, as
with all brokerage accounts, you will need to use the arbitration
process for this. It involves a hearing where a third party will make
the ultimate judgment on the case. If the evidence shows that you
misrepresented any information, you will likely lose the case.

The cash account form will also inquire if you are an insider
of any public corporation, which means that you own 10 percent or
more of the stock or that you have an executive-level position. Why
is this important? The reason is that you cannot short the stock of a
company for which you are an insider.

After you submit your cash account form, the brokerage firm
will want a minimum deposit. This varies from firm to firm, but the
minimum can range from $1,000 to $5,000. The deposit will first go
into a money market fund, where it will earn interest.

MARGIN ACCOUNT

A margin account allows you to borrow funds from your brokerage
firm. Basically, the cash and the securities in the margin account
serve as the collateral for the borrowing. There are many reasons

for taking out a margin loan. For example, you can use it to borrow money to make a consumer purchase, such as for a car or boat. Or, if you are having temporary cash flow problems, you can use the margin account for your cash needs—like paying the bills. Of course, the main reason for having a margin account is to borrow money to purchase stock. But it is also necessary to engage in short selling. The reason is that the margin account allows you to borrow shares from the brokerage firm.

While a typical consumer loan or credit card requires periodic payments of principal, this is not the case with a margin loan. Instead, the margin loan can last indefinitely, so long as the collateral in the account is sufficient. It is actually fairly common for investors to have ongoing margin loans. Yet, the investor will still need to pay monthly interest on the margin loan.

Because of the risks, margin accounts are highly regulated. This means that the process can be somewhat complicated. The main law for margin accounts is Regulation T (Reg T), which is part of the Securities and Exchange Act of 1934. Although, the Federal Reserve Board has the ultimate power to change the requirements, it is quite rare for this to happen. Many of the Regulation T requirements have not changed in decades. What's more, the brokerage industry has gone beyond these rules and has created their own protections. A critical one is that all securities in a margin account must be in "street name." Simply put, this means that the brokerage firm retains the stock certificates, which is actually the most common approach. This is beneficial to the investor because if you were to lose your stock certificates, it could be expensive and time-consuming to replace them.

By having securities in street name, the investor gets some important benefits. You can use limit orders and stop orders. These are sophisticated techniques to get a better price on a trade or to limit the downside of a position. Next, you should be able to get better updates from your brokerage firm. There is even insurance protection if the brokerage firm fails.

Another important rule for margin accounts is "hypothecation." Essentially, this means that you allow your broker to use the securities in your account for loans. At the same time, you will agree to "repothecation." This means that your broker will be able to use these securities to get loans from outside lending sources. All in all, the process of hypothecation and repothecation allows brokerage firms to facilitate short-selling transactions.

LEVERAGING YOUR PORTFOLIO

To understand margin accounts, it's important to see how they are used to purchase securities. For example: You think XYZ Corp. will increase in value over the next six months. You currently have $10,000 in your account. With XYZ Corp. trading at $100, you can purchase 100 shares. But what about buying 200 shares? With a margin account, you can. According to Regulation T, you may borrow up to 100 percent of the value of your unmargined assets in your portfolio and use this money to buy more shares. The formula for this is as follows:

Unmargined assets / 50%

Here's how it works: You place an order for 200 shares of XYZ Corp. In this case, the brokerage firm lends you $10,000 for the transaction, which becomes the debit balance. You then buy the other 100 shares with the $10,000 in your account. As a result, you would still have $10,000 in equity in your account.

Market Value	$20,000
Debit Balance	$10,000
Equity	$10,000

Suppose that your analysis was right and the shares of XYZ Corp. doubled. Your account would now look like this:

Market Value	$40,000
Debit Balance	$10,000
Equity	$30,000

As you can see, your initial $10,000 investment would increase by three times. Consider that without the leverage, the return would have been at only two times. But leverage can go both ways.

Let's say that XYZ Corp.'s shares fall to $50.

Market Value	$10,000
Debit Balance	$10,000
Equity	$0

Unfortunately, you would lose your initial $10,000 investment!

As you can see, the risks of margin trading are certainly substantial and this is why a brokerage firm will want to take precautions—which often exceed the requirements of Regulation T. Keep in mind that one of the causes of the stock market crash of 1929 was the high level of margin trading. Even the major financial problems of 2007–2008 were due, in large part, to the high levels of borrowing from investors.

Because of the risks of margin trading, a brokerage firm has the right to get a credit check on you, which is certainly reasonable. If you are denied an account because of the results of the report, you have the right to dispute this as well as get a copy of the report. It is common for there to be errors in credit reports.

GETTING "THE BORROW" AND INITIAL MARGIN REQUIREMENTS

When you decide to short a stock, you will need to make sure you can find shares to borrow. A brokerage firm's loan department handles this. They will either have the shares from existing margin accounts available or will seek them out from other firms. This is known as the "lending shares" market, and it is actually a big source of profits on Wall Street.

After you get shares to borrow, you next have to make sure you comply with the "initial margin requirements." Your account will actually have a subaccount for your short sales; this is done to make the process easier for the investor. According to Regulation T, the initial margin requirement is 50 percent of the short-sale proceeds.

So, for the amount you receive when you sell borrowed stock, there must be at least 50 percent of additional cash or securities set aside. This will appear as a *credit* in your margin account. Then, you will designate 100 percent of the short-sale proceeds as a credit in the margin account. This represents the collateral for the loan. Basically, this is money that you do not have access to—that is, until you cover the short position.

To understand this, let's take an example. Let's say that you short 100 shares of XYZ Corp. at a price of $50, which comes to $5,000. Under Regulation T, you will need to have at least $2,500 set aside in the margin account. What's more, you will need to deposit this amount "promptly." This is generally three business days—but no longer than five business days after the trade. If this requirement is not met, the broker can unwind the position.

Here's how the transaction will look in your margin account:

Transaction	Price	Proceeds	Margin Requirement	Credit Balance in Short Account
100 XYZ	$50.00	$5,000	$2,500	$5,000

At all times, you must have enough collateral in your account to at least cover the *current value* of your short position. If not, you will need to put up more cash or securities to bring up the level to 100 percent coverage. This is called "mark to market."

Suppose that the shares of XYZ Corp. increase to $60 and the value of your short position falls to $4,000. In this case, the brokerage would require you to post an additional $1,000. This would appear as a *debit* in your margin account.

What happens if the stock falls and goes to $50? Here, there would be a "reverse mark to market." You would receive a $1,000 credit in your account.

What if the value in the account increases because the shares of XYZ Corp. fall below $50? You would have an increase in buying power, which means you could get a higher loan to buy shares or to short stock.

Suppose that the shares of XYZ Corp. fall to $40. Your debit balance would now be $4,000 and you would have $1,000 in buying power. Under Regulation T, you have several options. First, you could take the $1,000 out of your account. This would increase the debit balance to $5,000 and you would have reached the maximum of the 50 percent under Regulation T. Next, you could buy $2,000 in more stock. This is because you could borrow an additional $1,000. The result is that the market value of the account would go to $12,000 and the debit balance would be $6,000. Finally, you could short $2,000 in more stock. As above, you could leverage the $1,000 in your account by two times the increase in value. This excess buying power is also called the "special memorandum account" or SMA. The excess $2,000 is added to this account.

No doubt, the short-selling process has many moving parts. This means that sometimes a brokerage firm will make errors. So it is a good idea to check all your trade confirmations. Are prices and amounts correct? If not, make sure you contact your firm immediately.

RESTRICTED ACCOUNT

The equity in a margin account is the difference between the market value and the credit balance and any amounts borrowed to purchase stock. But if the market value declines below the Regulation T's 50 percent requirement, then the account would be considered "restricted."

Suppose your account originally had a market value of $10,000 and a debit balance of $5,000. But over the next few months, the prices of the short position increase, bringing the market value down to $9,000. In this case, the account is below Regulation T. Even though the account is considered restricted, you could still short sell securities. However, to do this, you must provide more cash or securities in the account. Also, if you cover any short positions, 50 percent of the proceeds must go to reduce the debit balance.

COVERING A SHORT POSITION

Holding onto a short position can be costly, such as with your interest payments on the margin account. Because of this, short sellers often do not hold on to their positions for over a year.

The process of ending a short position is called "covering the short." This involves a multi-step process. Let's say that XYZ Corp. has gone from $50 to $30, which means you have a $2,000 gain. To cover the short, you would use your margin account to purchase 100 shares of the company for $3,000. The brokerage firm would then take possession of these securities and close out the short-sale position. When this happens, your margin account would no longer have money set aside as collateral. Instead, your account would have $2,000 more in cash. This would also be a credit, which could then be used to buy more shares or short stock.

MINIMUM MAINTENANCE REQUIREMENTS

What if the short-sale positions in your portfolio fall substantially? In this case, your brokerage firm will have safeguards. The key one is the so-called "minimum maintenance requirement." If you fall below this level, your brokerage firm will issue a "margin call," which is a demand for more cash or securities. If you fail to comply, then the firm can immediately sell the securities in your account.

For short selling, the minimum maintenance requirement is based on the stock price. The reason is that small-priced stocks are often volatile and can surge on good news. Moreover, they may be susceptible to a short squeeze, which could put further upward pressure on the stock price and increase the overall losses in the account.

The rules for short selling include the following:

- **For a stock selling below $5 per share:** The minimum maintenance requirement is $2.50 or 100 percent of the current market value, whichever is greater.
- **For a stock selling at $5 or above:** The minimum maintenance requirement is $5 per share or 30 percent of the current market value, whichever is greater.

To understand these rules, let's take a look at some examples. Say you buy 100 shares of XYZ Corp. at $4 each. The minimum maintenance requirement would be as follows:

$2.50 per share	$2.50 × 100 = $250
100% of current market value	$4.00 × 100 = $400

You must take the higher amount, which is $400. This would be the minimum maintenance requirement for the account.

Next, if the stock price is at $6, then here is the calculation:

$5.00 per share	$5 × 100 = $500
30% of current market value	30% × $600 = $180

You would select the one with $500.

MARGINABLE SECURITIES

Not all the assets in a margin account can be borrowed against. This is often the case with penny stocks. Typically, these shares have light trading volume and small market values, say below $100 million. But even if a stock is trading above this, it could still be tough to get margin loans. Rather, it is much easier if the market capitalization is over $1 billion. Brokerage firms will also be more comfortable providing margin loans for shares that trade on the main exchanges like the New York Stock Exchange (NYSE) or the Nasdaq. This would also include the top foreign exchanges. However, for the OTC Bulletin Board (OTCBB) and the Pink Sheets, a brokerage firm would likely be resistant.

An investor could also get loans against other assets. These include mutual funds, corporate bonds, and government bonds. Although, some types of investments are always nonmarginable. This is the case for options, annuities, money market funds, precious metals, and certificate of deposits. There are even certain accounts that do not allow margin trading—which, by definition, means that there is no short selling. These include Individual Retirement Accounts (IRAs), Uniform Gift to Minors Act accounts (UGMAs), and Uniform Transfer to Minors Act accounts (UTMAs).

TAXES AND SHORT SELLING

To lessen the impact of potential changes in the tax code, billionaire investor Edward Lampert considered distributing $864 million in stock to his investors in the ESL Partners hedge fund. He even took steps to transfer large share holdings into a "grantor retained annuity trust," which provides tax benefits when gifting to family members. The upshot would be millions of dollars in savings.[1]

These kinds of strategies are common for wealthy investors. But what about individual investors? Interestingly enough, they may miss out on major tax savings. Yet as taxes are likely to increase over time—because of the growing budget deficits—as

---

[1] http://www.bloomberg.com/news/2010-06-08lampert-may-avoid-obama-tax-increase-with-864-million-hedge-fund-payout.html.

well as the difficulty in generating strong returns, it definitely makes sense to use tax strategies.

When it comes to short selling, the IRS has special rules in terms of taxation. Unfortunately, they are not necessarily favorable (at least compared to long positions).

Tax matters are often convoluted and subject to change. It's also common for there to be differing interpretations on court decisions. This is certainly the case with the tax rules for short selling. So it is a good idea to seek professional advice on these matters. Yet it is still important to understand the fundamentals, so as to avoid problems and to take advantage of some of the tax breaks.

First of all, there are two types of tax rates. There are those for "capital gains," which are the profits on investments. If an investor holds onto the investment for over one year, then there are preferential tax rates for "long-term capital gains." These tax rates range from 10 percent to 15 percent. If the investment holding period is less than a year, the investor must use the ordinary tax rates for "short-term capital gains." These tax rates range from 10 percent to 35 percent. Thus, investors try to find ways to get long-term capital gains, so as to qualify for the lower rates.

To calculate a capital gain or loss, you use the following formula:

Amount Realized – Adjusted Basis = Gain or Loss

For a long position, this is easy. Suppose that you purchase 100 shares of XYZ Corp. at $50 and pay a $10 commission. Your adjusted basis would be $5,010 (100 shares times $50 plus $10 commission). Then the stock increases to $60 and you sell your position. Your amount realized would be $5,990 (you need to subtract the $10 commission), and your capital gain would be $980. Assuming you held onto the stock for over a year, the capital gains tax would be $147 or 15 percent times $980.

Now suppose you shorted XYZ Corp. and the price fell to $40. You would reverse the calculation. The initial transaction would result in the amount realized of $4,990. Then a year goes by and you would cover the position. This means your adjusted basis would be $4,010. The result is that you would have a capital gain of $980. So this means it is a long-term capital gain and the tax is $147? The answer is no. The holding period is really just the few seconds it took to buy the stock! It sounds harsh, but this is how the IRS looks at the matter. In other words, the transaction would be taxed at the higher ordinary tax rates.

SHORTING AGAINST THE BOX

If you have a gain in a stock, you could use short selling to lock it in. This is known as "shorting against the box." For example, suppose you purchased 100 shares of XYZ Corp. at $50. A few months go by and the stock surges to $70. You still think the stock has a good long-term future but you are concerned about the next quarterly report. It seems likely that the company will miss the Wall Street estimates and the stock price will fall, so you decide to short 100 shares of XYZ Corp. at $70. By doing this, you cannot make any more on the trade or lose any more. The long and short positions offset each other. It is essentially the perfect hedge.

While this makes sense from an investment perspective, it could have negative tax consequences. The IRS may consider the short sale to be a "constructive sale" of your long position. This means you would have to pay taxes on the $20 capital gain. But there are exceptions. First, the rule does not apply if the long position has not increased in value. This means there will be no recognition of a capital loss. But of course, shorting against the box is typically for those investors who want to protect a gain. Next, there is no constructive sale if you are meeting a timing rule and close the short position no longer than 30 days after the start of the year and hold the stock—without the short position—for 60 days.

Let's look into this concept in a little more detail. Say that on November 10, you buy 100 shares of XYZ Corp. at $50. On December 31, you have a gain of $20 per share and short 100 shares against the box. Then on January 20, you cover your short position. You also keep your 100-share long position for another 60 days. In this case, there is no constructive sale of the stock. As you can see, it is important to keep track of the timing on this kind of transaction. It is certainly easy to miss the deadlines.

Finally, some investors will try to avoid the constructive sale rule by shorting a stock that is *similar* to the long position. For example, suppose you have a gain in United Airlines. To protect this, you short the shares of American Airlines. For the most part, this should avoid any tax problems. However, this is not a perfect hedge. It is possible that the two stocks will diverge, such as because of bad management decisions. In other words, the shares of United Airlines may fall and the shares of American Airlines may rise, which means you may wind up with an overall loss on the strategy.

WORTHLESS STOCK

It's the ultimate for any short seller: a stock that becomes worthless. You get to keep the total proceeds from the original sale and you have doubled your money. But what happens from a tax perspective? The answer is that—on the day the shares become worthless—you must recognize the gain or loss.

Yet, there is some ambiguity; that is, what is "worthless"? There are examples where a company falls into bankruptcy and the shares are trading for pennies. But there is still value. In fact, this may last for many years. As a result, a short seller can avoid paying taxes until the stock is officially worthless, which means the stock no longer trades.

THE WASH-SALE RULE

You can deduct your capital losses against your capital gains. And, if there are still more left, you can deduct up to as much as $3,000 in capital losses against ordinary income. Because of the higher tax rates, this is definitely a nice tax benefit. But you may not deduct capital losses if you violate the "wash-sale rule." This is when you buy substantially identical securities within 30 days before or after the date of sale. The main reason is that the IRS does not want taxpayers to avoid paying capital gains taxes by taking in-and-out trades.

The wash-sale rule also applies to short selling. However, it can be somewhat complicated. So to make things easier, let's use an example. You buy 100 shares of XYZ Corp. for $50. Two months later, you short 100 shares of the same company at $40 and then a couple of months later, you buy an additional 100 shares for the same price. Then within 15 days, you cover your short by delivering 100 shares of XYZ Corp. In this case, you claim a loss because the 100 shares you used were purchased at $50 apiece and the short position was taken at $40. But, the IRS would not agree. The agency would consider that you really did not make any substantive changes in your position. As a result, you would not get to take a loss because of the wash-sale rule.

DIVIDENDS

If you short a stock that pays dividends, then you must reimburse these payments to your brokerage firm. In terms of taxes, you may be eligible for a deduction. This is so if you itemize your deductions. What's more, you can only deduct up to the amount of net interest income you generate for the year (which also includes annuities and royalties).

Another restriction is if you cover your short position within 45 days of the initial short sale. However, even if this situation transpires, you will be able to add the dividend payments to your adjusted basis. This will ultimately mean a lower gain on your transaction, which will translate into tax savings.

Finally, you need to be aware of "extraordinary dividends." This is at least 10 percent of the amount of proceeds from the short sale. If you receive an extraordinary dividend, you will not be able to deduct it unless you keep the short position for more than a year.

INVESTMENT INTEREST

According to IRS terminology, the interest you pay on your margin account is called "investment interest." However, the agency has strict requirements on the deductibility of this type of expense. First, the interest must be for borrowed money used for investments. In this situation, short selling does qualify. Next, you can deduct the interest up to the amount of your net investment income. For any excess, you can carry forward the amounts to future tax years.

All in all, these rules are far from easy. Again, this is why it's important to keep track of your trading activities as well as get the help of a tax expert who understands the intricacies of short selling. In the next chapter, we will take a look at some of the risks of short selling, which go beyond making a wrong bet on a stock. As you will see, short selling has unique risk like short squeezes and buy-ins.

CHAPTER 3

Risks and Costs of Short Selling

Key Concepts

- The impact from bid-ask spreads
- The costs of margin interest
- The risks of short squeezes and unlimited losses

For many investors, the short-selling process takes some time to understand. But this is fine. Often even experienced brokers will not have a strong grasp of this investment technique. The fact remains that the stock market has a strong bias for long positions.

The good news is that with electronic brokerage trading, it is much easier to engage in short selling. Once your margin account is set up, it may be just a matter of a few clicks to pull off a trade. But this can lull an investor into complacency. Short selling certainly has a variety of risks. And in some cases, the losses can be substantial. Even top short sellers have taken big hits to their portfolios. So investors need to understand the key risks before making any short-sale trades. What's more, there should also be risk management, which is covered in Chapter 16.

THE BID-AND-ASK SPREAD

Often overlooked, the bid-and-ask spread can be a material cost for a short seller (as well as for a buyer of shares). To understand this, here's a typical quote:

Stock	Last Trade	Bid	Ask
Google	470.30	469.92 × 500	471.50 × 500

Google's stock is traded on the Nasdaq exchange, which is essentially an electronic marketplace. When you short a stock, you will sell it at the "bid price." Based on the quote, a "market maker" is willing to buy 500 shares at $469.92 each. This is a financial firm that is a member of the Nasdaq and will take the other side of a trade. The *profit* is the difference between the "bid price" and the "ask price." But this is a *cost* to the outside investor. So when you short Google at $469.92, you will not break even on the trade until the ask price hits this price.

The New York Stock Exchange (NYSE) also has a bid-ask spread, but on the NYSE, there are no market makers. Instead, the financial firms that facilitate the trading are called "specialists" and they conduct their transactions on a physical trading floor.

With trading in large stocks like Exxon and Microsoft, the bid-ask spread is minimal. The reason is that these shares have a tremendous amount of liquidity. But when you look at small-cap stocks—especially those with market values below $500 million or so—the spread can be large and represent a cut in your potential profits. Of course, a good source for short-sale ideas is in the small-cap sector. So what should you do? Through your broker or online account, you should attempt to get a price within the bid-ask spread (this is known as a "limit order"). While this does not always work, it is certainly worth a try.

MARGIN INTEREST AND COMMISSIONS

As seen in Chapter 2, you need to set up a margin account when you sell short stock. This also means you will have to pay interest on any amount that you borrow for the transaction. This will include the initial debit balance as well as additional debit balances if the short position falls in value.

Margin rates depend primarily on the amount of the margin loan in the account. What's more, the rates change daily based on current interest rates. Here's an example of the margin rates for E*TRADE during July 11, 2010:

Table 3.1

Margin Rates for E*Trade, July 11, 2010

Debit Balance	Margin Rate
$1,000,000 or more	3.89%
$500,000 to $999,999	4.14%
$250,000 to $499,999.99	5.14%
$100,000 to $249,999.99	6.14%
$50,000 to $99,999.99	7.14%
$25,000 to $49,999.99	7.64%
Less than $24,999.99	8.14%

For each short-sale trade, you will also need to pay a commission. This should be no different from what you would pay for a long position. If a brokerage has a different rate, you should go to a rival firm. The commission for a short-sale transaction is based on various factors including the number of shares, the stock price, and the level of trading volume. You will generally pay a higher commission for less-liquid stock. There may also be some fees, which are a part of your margin account. These are often for noncompliance and the fees generally range from $10 to $50 or so. Examples include checks returned for nonsufficient funds, margin calls, late trade settlements, and worthless securities processing.

An investor must also factor in a variety of hidden costs. One is collateral. Since a short seller must have 100 percent set aside for a trade, this locks up capital, which could be used for other investment opportunities. What's more, if the value of a short-sale position falls in value, you will need to put up more money in the margin account.

Then dividends are a problem. When a short seller borrows shares, the lender still has the rights to any dividends. So the short seller actually must pay the dividend amounts to the lender. As a result, short sellers will often avoid dividend-paying stocks.

Finally, a short seller has limited shareholder rights. After all, he or she does not have any ownership in the shares. This means the short seller will not be able to vote on important corporate matters or get equity interests from spin-offs or rights offerings.

SIPC COVERAGE

What if your brokerage firm fails? What will happen to your short positions? Just as with your long positions, you will be covered by the "Securities Investor Protection Corporation" (SIPC). This is a non-profit corporation that insures the amounts in your brokerage account. The maximum coverage is $500,000 per account. Of this, only $100,000 is in cash. But keep in mind that the insurance does not guard against market volatility. Instead, it is a way to deal with the rare event where a brokerage firm lacks liquidity and must shut down.

Brokerage firms will often get excess insurance coverage. Depending on the size and changes in your account, make sure you are adequately covered. You can access more information about the SIPC at http://www.sipc.org.

UNLIMITED LOSSES

There's an old saying on Wall Street: "When you short a stock, the potential losses are unlimited, but the most you can profit is 100 percent." This is definitely a grim statement. But as with any time-honored quote, it has shades of truth.

First of all, it is correct that the most you can make is 100 percent. This is the amount of the initial short-sale position. But of course, it is rare for a company's stock to go to zero. Instead, most short sellers look for short-term gains of 10 percent to 20 percent or so.

Next, it is theoretically possible to have unlimited losses. Just imagine if you had shorted the stock of Microsoft when it first went public in 1987. If you had held onto the short, you would have lost a staggering amount. But this is an unlikely scenario. Keep in mind that your broker would have likely unwound your short-sale trade.

LITIGATION COSTS

This section is mostly for major investors, such as those who manage hedge funds. Yes, some investors will sue a company that they have a short position in. Shareholders have a right to bring litigation against a company if there is a case of fraud. These are known as "derivative lawsuits," and they have actually become quite common over the past two decades. On the other hand, a company may bring a lawsuit against a vocal short seller. Interestingly enough, such a lawsuit may be a red flag that the company really does have something to hide.

In some cases, a short seller will even spread a false rumor to gain from a short-sale position. For example, Mark Jakob used a newswire site on the Internet to spread a false story that the chief executive officer (CEO) of Emulex was leaving. Jakob made $241,000 on the trade. Or, there was the case where several investors spread a false report that Sea World's Shamu was ill. Needless to say, these activities are illegal; they are often called "distort and short." The SEC has gone after these types of short sellers—even though their profits were relatively small.

THE BORROW

Even if you have identified a great short-sale target, you may not be able to make the transaction because of the peculiarities of margin accounts. One problem is that a security may not meet the requirements for a margin account. This is typically the case because of light trading volume or the riskiness of the company. Another issue is when the stock is a "hot commodity." In other words, many short sellers are taking a position in the company. When this happens, a brokerage firm may actually give preference to top clients, such as hedge funds. Then from time to time, there may be minimal shares in margin accounts. In fact, this could be the result of the company. How?

Consider the software maker Microstrategy. When the stock price was plunging, the CEO wrote a letter to shareholders to take their certificates out of street name. The result was that it became extremely difficult to short the stock.

ROARING BULL MARKETS

In a typical bull market, a short seller can make money. It is common for there to be small drops as well as corrections. Besides, there are always companies that fail to execute on their strategy or even engage in fraud. But when the markets are in a bubble, it can be almost impossible to get returns. The reason is that—when the markets reach a speculative point—it seems that every stock increases in value, regardless of the quality.

This has happened during various periods throughout U.S. history, such as the 1920s and 1990s. Typically, some type of transformative change in technology is driving the bull market. In the 1920s, it was radio and in the 1990s, it was the Internet. The problem is that it can be extremely difficult to predict the fall of a roaring bull market. Actually, such a phase can easily last for several years. And this is long enough to result in substantial losses for a short seller.

Even famed short seller Jim Chanos suffered tremendously during the 1990s. For example, he aggressively shorted high-fliers like AOL. But his analysis did not matter—even though he was eventually proved correct when the bubble burst. As a result, Chanos saw his short-only fund lose about three-quarters of its value from 1991 to 1999.

THE BUY-IN

When you establish a margin account, you agree to a "buy-in." This means that your brokerage firm can require you to cover a short at any time, for any reason. This happens if the brokerage firm decides to sell the shares and does not have enough available to cover existing short positions. Needless to say, this can cause much frustration for a client. Because of this, a brokerage firm will try to avoid a buy-in situation. And if a brokerage firm has no choice but to initiate a buy-in, there is a temptation to focus on smaller clients, who do not generate as much business.

SHORT SQUEEZE

In the short-selling game, there are a variety of scary-sounding concepts. Perhaps one of the most ominous is the "short squeeze," which involves a stock that has a heavy concentration of short-sale positions. The problem is when there is a spike in the stock price, such as because of a positive earnings release or a new deal. When this happens, the short sellers will rush to "cover" their positions. This means they will buy more and more shares. In other words, the stock will continue to surge, which will magnify the losses.

Depending on the volume of the stock and the number of shares shorted, it can take several days to a few months for short sellers to substantially unload their positions and the stock price to come back to reasonable levels. But in the meantime, it can be harrowing for investors. In fact, a short seller may have little choice but to cover because of a buy-in.

Perhaps one of the most infamous cases of a short squeeze happened in 2008. The company was Volkswagen. Going into 2008, the auto industry was having major problems because of the recession. Yet the stock price of Volkswagen continued to increase steadily, so hedge funds—like SAC Capital, Greenlight Capital, and Glenview Capital—started to take a large short position in the stock. However, because of a quirk in the German securities laws, Porsche had been buying up the stock in Volkswagen. By October 2008, Porsche said it owned roughly 94.2 percent of the company's outstanding shares.

The problem was that the short sellers had shorted a whopping 12 percent. In other words, there were not enough shares to cover the position and the stock price of Volkswagen surged. The market cap reached $456 billion, making the company the most valuable in the world. The losses totaled in the billions. And the most tragic case was Adolf Merckle. At 74, he had an estimated fortune of $9.2 billion. But because of his short position—and the onset of the credit crisis—he had a liquidity problem. So he was forced to sell off his assets and saw his fortune evaporate. In his home town of Blaubeuren, he stepped in front of a train and committed suicide.

While this is certainly an extreme case, the fact is that a short squeeze is a big risk for any short seller. The good news is that there are tools to help you avoid the problem. First, there is the "short-interest ratio." This shows the number of days it would take to cover all the short positions. The formula is:

Short Interest / Average Daily Volume

Generally, if this comes to five or more days, then a stock could be vulnerable to a short squeeze. Next, a short seller will use the "float percentage indicator." This is a modification of the short-interest ratio and is calculated as follows:

Short Interest / Float

Often investors confuse float with outstanding shares, but they are clearly different. The "outstanding shares" are the total number owned by investors. The "float," on the other hand, is the number of shares that can be sold without restriction. Keep in mind that public companies often have selling restrictions on major shareholders and senior officers. A short seller often focuses on the float since this is a much more accurate gauge of the liquidity of a stock. So if the short interest is a large percentage of the float—say more than 10 percent—then there could be a high risk of a short squeeze.

BEFORE A SHORT SQUEEZE

Interestingly enough, a stock price may fall steadily before a short squeeze. The reason is that bearish investors are taking larger short positions in this stock. This is actually creating more shares on the market and is likely to put downward pressure on the stock. How? Let's look at a simple example.

Suppose XYZ Corp. has four investors and they each own 10,000 shares. The current stock price is $40 and the total market value is $1,600,000 (40,000 shares × $40). Then you take a short position in XYZ Corp. for 10,000 shares. Where do these shares come from? You need to borrow them from existing investors, who have shares in a margin account. But consider that you had to sell 10,000 shares for the short sale. In other words, there are now 10,000 extra shares in the market, or a total of 50,000. But if there has been no fundamental change in XYZ Corp., then the share price will need to fall to equate the $1,600,000 market value or $32 per share. However, you will eventually need to cover your short sale, which means buying back the 10,000 shares. When this happens, the stock price should go back up and the outstanding shares will then fall back to 40,000 shares.

MERGERS AND ACQUISITIONS

A common strategy for companies to grow is to pull off mergers and acquisitions. But this can be bad news for short sellers. The main reason is that, in most cases, an acquisition is at a premium to the current stock price. In fact, it can easily be 40 percent or over. Needless to say, this can lead to a terrible loss in a short position. To this end, short sellers try to avoid companies that are the subject of acquisition rumors. Also, they may avoid those industries that are currently undergoing consolidation.

Note: Short sellers are careful with biotech companies, especially those that are close to receiving Food and Drug Administration (FDA) approval. If a drug gets clearance, the stock price is likely to surge.

THE UPTICK RULE

Back in 1938, Congress investigated short selling to see if there was manipulation. The result was that the Securities and Exchange Commission (SEC) enacted the "uptick rule." It essentially allowed short selling under two conditions:

- **A transaction on a + tick:** This is when the most recent trade is higher than the preceding trade.
- **A transaction on a 0+ tick:** This is when the current price is the same one as the preceding trade.

An example of a 0+ tick would be when a stock goes from $20.00 to $20.20 to $20.20.

The belief was that the uptick rule would blunt speculative short-selling activity and reduce overall volatility. But by 2007, the SEC decided to repeal the rule. The rationale was that the uptick rule increased friction in markets and reduced liquidity. Yet there was still much controversy. Some companies—which saw steep declines in their stock prices—thought that the lack of the uptick rule was a big problem. Then, with the 2007–2008 financial panic, the debate intensified and even became a political issue. The 2008 Republican candidate for president, Senator John McCain, said the uptick rule made the stock market into a "casino."[1]

By 2009, the SEC put the matter to a public comment and has even made several proposals.[2] First, there is the market-wide, permanent approach. Yes, this is a mouthful (and shows how complicated these issues can get). The proposal has two options. One is simply to reenact the uptick rule. The other is to enact a modified uptick rule. This accounts for the problems of modern trading. Consider that with millions of trades, there are often delays in the reporting. This makes it extremely difficult to get accurate pre-trade levels. To deal with this, a modified uptick rule would be focused on a national bid price.

If these two options are not sufficient, the SEC offered the idea of a "circuit breaker." Again, this has two forms. First of all, there could be a ban of short selling for the day if there has been a large drop in the stock. Or there could be a partial ban. That is, if the stock increases above a national bid, short selling would be permitted. While it is not clear what the outcome will be, it is certainly a reasonable possibility that there will be some type of price-restriction on short selling.

SHORT-SELLING BANS

In September 2008, the SEC used its emergency powers to enact a ban on the short selling of roughly 800 financial company stocks. The ban expired on October 8, 2008. It was an extraordinary decision. Consider that the last time there was a ban in the United States was in 1931, when there were concerns about the dismantling of the gold standard in the United Kingdom. But when markets are undergoing extreme volatility, investors will often blame the short sellers. And in late 2008, there was definitely much fear and uncertainty. Even top companies, like Goldman Sachs and Morgan Stanley, saw steep declines in their stock prices. The hope was that a temporary ban would help provide breathing room.

---

[1] http://online.wsj.com/article/SB122175692668652881.html.

[2] http://sec.gov.rules/proposed/2009/34-59748.pdf.

Did it work? It is still early to get good conclusions but there are already some academic studies on the matter. One is entitled "Shackling Short Sellers: The 2008 Shorting Ban."[3] The authors include professors from Columbia University, Cornell, and Texas A&M. The study showed that there was indeed a plunge in short-selling activity on the ban list, which went from 12.47 percent of volume to 1.96 percent. Why didn't the volume go to zero? Keep in mind that the SEC allowed market makers to continue to short the market so as to provide liquidity. All in all, stocks on the ban list experienced higher returns compared to the markets. In some cases, the spikes were significant. For example, the shares of Fannie Mae (Federal National Mortgage Association or FNMA) went from 50 cents to about $2 per share. But after the ban, the shares went back down to 60 cents.

Again, a ban on short selling is a rare event. But, it is definitely a risk for short sellers. The likely result will be a surge in the stock prices, which will mean lower returns.

LITTLE RISK FOR WALL STREET FIRMS?

Many Wall Street firms have a securities lending division. This allows them to pool the securities in margin accounts that can be lent to short sellers. This is a highly profitable business, especially since many of the customers are hedge funds. To understand this, let's take a look at the overall process.

Suppose ABC Strategies, which is a top hedge fund, has spotted XYZ Corp. as a good short-sale prospect. The company's revenues have been falling and the competitive environment is getting tougher. Like any short seller, ABC Strategies needs to borrow shares from a brokerage firm. Often, this is the prime brokerage arm of a Wall Street firm, like Goldman Sachs, Bank of America, and Morgan Stanley. Let's say that ABC Strategies' prime brokerage is X1 Trading. The firm essentially provides a turnkey platform for the hedge fund. The services include processing of trades, software tools to track the performance of the portfolio, and risk management services. In fact, X1 Trading even leases some of its offices and computer terminals to ABC Strategies. Of course, the services

---

[3] http://www.2.gsb.columbia.edu/faculty/cjones/ShortingBan.pdf.

result in hefty fees for X1 Trading. But for a hedge fund, the benefits are usually worth it. It would simply cost too much to build this
type of infrastructure. Besides, a hedge fund wants to focus on
ways of generating strong returns.

All in all, more than a majority of a prime brokerage's transaction processing will be from long positions. But, there is still a
large amount of short-sale trades—and they can be quite lucrative.
So a prime brokerage firm will pool its securities in margin
accounts and lend them to hedge funds. If they run short on securities, they will then call on other prime brokerages to find supply.
It is a multibillion-dollar market, which has hefty fees for the prime
brokerages. What's more, the risk of these loans is virtually zero.
The reason is that a hedge fund must have 100 percent collateral
against each trade. Also, when a position declines in value, there
must be an increase in the collateral posted.

During rare times, however, there can be risk. This is the case
during financial panics. A hedge fund may have difficulty selling
its positions because there are essentially no ready buyers. When
this happens, there may not be a payback on the loans. This was the
fear in 2008. It was not uncommon for hedge funds to move large
amounts of money out of their prime brokerage accounts.
Interestingly, it was such activity that contributed to the collapse of
Bear Stearns and Lehman Brothers. Even top prime brokerage
operators, such as Morgan Stanley and Goldman Sachs, suffered
tremendous losses. But again, the hedge funds needed a place to
put their money. To this end, they moved their money over to the
largest financial firms including Credit Suisse, Deutsche Bank, and
JP Morgan Chase.

So even for the largest players, there are significant risks to
short selling. But so long as they are understood and monitored,
the benefits of short selling are too great to pass up. Short selling is
certainly a major profit driver for sophisticated investors like
hedge funds—and this is increasingly becoming the case for individual investors. So in the next chapter, we will take the first steps
on how to find a good short-sale candidate.

CHAPTER 4

Fundamental Analysis

Key Concepts

- Spotting fads and failed business models
- Looking for catalysts
- Types of stocks to short

The best short sellers use painstaking research and analysis. In some cases, the effort can be enormous. Consider that hedge fund manager Bill Ackman analyzed roughly 140,000 pages of documents when he shorted MBIA. Yet investors do not have to go to these efforts to be successful. If anything, research has gotten easier over the years because of the Internet. Just a quick search on Google can produce valuable information. For example, a short seller can learn about the competition, industry trends, management backgrounds, fads, and so on. While there may not necessarily be any "smoking guns," the fact is that this information will help the short seller build an investment thesis.

COMPETITION

A hallmark of any free market system is competition. It is natural and healthy. Competition allows for more innovation and choice for consumers—as well as lower prices. Of course, competition can be particularly tough for companies. This is why Warren Buffett looks for companies that have "moats." This is a way of saying that there are powerful barriers to entry. For example, Buffett purchased Burlington Northern Santa Fe because the railroad industry has long-term growth prospects and competition will be fairly light. The reasons include the huge expense in creating an alternative railroad and the lack of lower-cost competition from China or India.

However, many companies do not have moats. Rather, when these companies start to see success, new rivals quickly come into the market, which in turn causes growing pressure on sales and profits. This is something that gets the keen attention of short sellers—but the overall market may miss this. Short sellers may think that the company will find ways to grow despite the competition or that the company will launch new innovative products and leverage its brand. Because of this, the stock price may stay fairly high—even though there is deterioration. For a short seller, this provides an opportunity to build a position in the stock and get nice returns.

A short seller will also look for competition that represents a disruption to the leader in the industry. This causes the "innovator's dilemma." This is when a new technology greatly improves the product and makes it nearly impossible for the leader to fight back. The reason is that it is too costly to restructure its operations.

A recent example is Blockbuster Video. Interestingly enough, the company was an early innovator in specialty retailing and enjoyed the surge in video and DVD sales. But a new player came onto the scene in the late 1990s: NetFlix. This company's model was highly disruptive, since it offered more choice and convenience. What's more, it did not have to deal with the huge costs of a retail infrastructure. Eventually, the stock of Blockbuster had to be delisted from the Nasdaq.

Another type of competitive threat that short sellers will look at is deregulation. Some types of industries are known as "natural monopolies." This is when a product or service is essential, such as an electric utility. What's more, competition would actually harm consumers. The reason is that it would be costly and inefficient to have multiple infrastructures. The federal government allows natural monopolies but imposes restrictions, such as on pricing and contract terms. The upshot is that the returns are steady, regardless of the economic environment. To break out of this, some companies will diversify into other industries. When this happens, short sellers get interested. Is a company that is highly regulated—and has a history of little competition—prepared to take on rivals? As seen in the utilities industry, the answer is often "no." The result is that there can actually be sharp reductions in the stock prices of companies that would normally be stable.

On the other hand, the federal government may deregulate an industry. This will mean new competitors will come into the sector. In many cases, the existing operators will have difficulties in dealing with the pressures. An example is the airline industry, which was deregulated in the late 1970s.

Finally, some companies will try to deal with competition by building a portfolio of patents. A company will file a patent with the federal government, which gives it an exclusive right to use the technology for 18 years. A patent can essentially guarantee a competition-free market. This can be quite effective for the biotech and pharmaceutical industries. But for many other industries, patents have an elusive ability to protect markets. First of all, some countries have little enforcement of patents. Next, a patent can be avoided with differences in engineering.

THE COMMODITY TRAP

A "commodity" is a product that has no differentiation. Because of this, the price should be the same. Some companies have turned commodities into offerings that customers will actually pay a premium, for example, Starbucks and coffee. Another case is Apple, which turned commodities—cell phone devices and MP3 players—into high-margin products. But in hypercompetitive global markets, it is common for premium products to eventually become commodities. When this happens, profits collapse and so do the stock prices.

Some short sellers will look for this transition, which often requires a strong understanding of the industry. Take a look at the providers of navigation devices. Since the early 1990s, these companies enjoyed strong growth as consumers and businesses realized the value of the products. But as time went by, it got easier to develop GPS technologies. For example, Google developed its own

platform and made it available for free. It was the ultimate technology disruption and it had a devastating impact on GPS companies like Garmin and TomTom.

CUSTOMER CONCENTRATION

Customer concentration is common in Corporate America, especially for industries where there are not many potential buyers. An
example is the auto supply market. However, there is no clear-cut
standard for customer concentration. If a large percentage of
sales—say more than 30 percent—come from five customers or so,
then there is a risk and short sellers will take note. One reason is
that the company will not have much leverage. For example, a customer can better negotiate prices because the company does not
want to lose the account.

Also, the loss of an existing customer can be enormous. Just
look at Digital River, which provides e-commerce services to the
software industry. In 2009, close to 24 percent of revenues came
from Symantec. Unfortunately, the company said it would build its
own system—to lower its costs. As a result, Digital River's stock
price plunged 38 percent on the news.

FADS

A "fad" is often a favorite for short sellers. By definition, these are
trends that will eventually fizzle out. And when this happens, the
results can be terrible for a company's stock price. Sales and profits plunge. But if this happens, it is often too quick to take effective
actions. It is not uncommon for fad companies to ultimately wind
up in bankruptcy.

There is one key issue here to keep in mind; that is, a fad may
really be the beginning of a new industry. Over the years, such
things as radio, television, fast food, personal computers, and the
Internet were considered fads. Of course, they turned into mega-
trends that changed industries. Yet there *are* some areas that are
prone to fads. One area is the restaurant industry. It seems that
every year there is a new concept, which gets lots of buzz. Then
within a few years, the consumer gets bored and moves on to the
next exciting thing. At the same time, the restaurant industry has

relatively low margins and often attracts many imitators. Just take a look at the bagel phenomenon during the 1990s. Earlier players like Einstein's Bagels saw tremendous success. But it was not an easily defendable idea. So a slew of competitors entered the market, taking down industry profits. By 2001, the shares of Einstein's Bagels were selling at only five cents.

Another market that is susceptible to fads is technology. Since the 1960s, the U.S. stock markets have seen many new technologies catch the attention of investors; but only a few of these companies have survived. Some of those that failed include Atari, Wang Computers, Osborne Computer, Commodore, and so on.

A more likely scenario is for a tech company to have one hot product but be unable to come up with another one. Yes, these are tech one-hit wonders. And once the hot-product loses steam, the company's shares can languish for many years. One example is Novell. During the 1980s, the company built a fast-growing industry in networking. But by the 1990s, Microsoft entered the market and eventually became the dominant player. Despite a variety of new products and acquisitions, Novell was never able to get back on the growth ramp again.

If a company relies mostly on one product, this is certainly a sign that there will be trouble. One example is Happiness Express. Its flagship product—the Mighty Morphin Power Rangers—was growing at a rapid clip. Then, it represented a whopping 80 percent of profits. When the fad died out in the mid-1990s, so did Happiness Express, which had to file for bankruptcy. Indeed, the toy industry as a whole is particularly susceptible to fads. Let's face it, kids are notoriously fickle—and get bored easily.

Even though these industries have a high probability of experiencing fads, a short seller still needs to do more analysis. A fad can easily last for several years. Thus, it is important to find signs that the fad is coming to an end, and there are several approaches to doing so. First, a big red flag is when the company misses its sales and earnings forecast, especially when this happens during the strong quarter of the year. Another danger is when there has been a recent drop in prices or an increase in incentives and promotions. Basically, the company is having troubles moving inventory. And speaking of inventory, a short seller will track this closely. Is it growing faster than sales?

REGULATORY ACTIONS

Over the years, the United States has established a growing number of regulations to prevent and punish fraud. These include extensive disclosures, increased investigations, and higher fines and jail sentences. But such measures can only go so far. The fact remains that some company managements will continue to violate regulations or even break criminal laws.

If caught, the consequences can be long-lasting for a company. First, key managers will leave the company and there will be a need to find replacements, which is not easy. It can certainly be a big distraction for the company. There's also a good chance that business will slow down. After all, a key to a company's success has to do with its aggressive strategies. But if a government agency takes actions against this and even prevents these practices, there could be a slowdown in revenues.

One example is the antitrust case against Microsoft. Over the years, the company enjoyed a monopoly in the PC operating systems market, which generated huge amounts of cash flows. This allowed Microsoft to aggressively move into other software categories, such as with its Office Suite. But the federal government believed Microsoft had too much market power, which enabled it to get major concessions. As a result, the company has had to deal with a variety of restrictions. In fact, the company's stock has been a relative poor performer ever since.

A short seller will also take notice of safety violations and other serious regulatory violations. Perhaps the most telling example is BP, which had to spend billions of dollars because of the oil spill in the Gulf of Mexico. Keep in mind that prior to the oil spill BP had one of the worst safety records in the industry.

DELAYED FINANCIALS

Public companies are required to make periodic reports. This can be expensive, costing millions of dollars per year in fees for attorneys, auditors, and accountants. But if a company is unable to produce its financials in a timely manner, then short sellers will get interested. There may be several reasons for this. One may be that there are problems with internal controls and procedures. Or, the company may be under investigation and there may be a question if its reports are accurate.

The delay may ultimately mean that a company will have to issue a "restatement." This means that prior financials failed to meet regulatory requirements. Needless to say, this concerns investors and the stock price usually falls. A restatement may eventually be followed by sanctions from the SEC. This can easily take a year or two. So there may be a second opportunity for short sellers to make a profit on the trade.

UNEXPECTED LOSS

For the most part, a company will provide enough guidance for analysts to come up with reasonable earnings' estimates. But in some cases a company will have a "big miss." The worst is when a company posts an unexpected large loss—when the Wall Street consensus expected a profit. What happened? It could possibly be a one-time event. But short sellers are likely to be skeptical. Bear in mind that companies usually have a variety of ways to make up shortfalls—at least in terms of avoiding a big miss.

So if a company cannot soften an unexpected loss, it could mean that there is a fundamental problem with the business. This may cause the share price to continue to deteriorate.

DIVIDEND CUTS

One of the main duties of a company's board of directors is to decide whether or not to declare a dividend. This is a big responsibility. After all, some shareholders rely on dividends for their income. Thus, if the board decides to cut the dividend—or even eliminate it—then short sellers are alerted. Is the company having cash-flow problems?

Actually, there is a technique to help predict a dividend cut. This involves two things. First, a short seller will look at the Earnings per Share (EPS) percentage. This is the ratio of the dividend to the EPS. If this is 90 percent or higher, then there is a risk of a cut. Next, a short seller will see if a company has a high yield, when compared to its peers. When this happens, a company may be pressured to cut back on the dividend because of the drain on cash flows.

STOCK SPLIT AND REVERSE SPLIT

A "stock split" is when a company issues more shares to bring the stock price down. The reason? This is to make the shares more affordable for smaller investors.

The general approach is for a 2–for–1 split. This means that for every share you own, you will get another one. The result is that the price of the shares will fall by one-half. But there is also a "reverse split." This is when a company takes back shares; it does this to boost the stock price. Often, the ratios will be quite high, for example, a 1-for-15 split. This is because the stock price is usually extremely low—generally under a dollar.

While a reverse split does not change the fundamentals of a company, it is nonetheless a signal for short sellers that management believes that the stock may continue to go lower. So why not try to boost it now? What's more, a reverse split may indicate that a company is more concerned about public relations and hype to boost the stock price—not necessarily the lingering problems of sales and profits. A study from a professor at the Houston State University shows that from 1950 to 2000, the companies that had reverse splits saw their stock price fall by an average of a third within three years.[1]

THE END OF GROWTH

Every growth company has its limits. And when they are reached, there is usually a fall in the stock price. In fact, the fall can be significant as growth investors flee the stock and move elsewhere.

Short sellers call this the "law of large numbers." Simply put, this means that—as revenues get large—it becomes tougher and tougher to generate new growth. For example, if a company is at $20 billion in revenues and has been traditionally growing at 30 percent per year, then it will need to post a whopping $6 billion in revenues for the next 12 months. Clearly, this is extremely difficult and many companies will stumble. This predicament has been the case with many former growth companies, like Cisco, Intel, and Microsoft.

---

[1] http://www.rdboehme.com/Papers/fire_180.pdf.

Short sellers look for signs that companies have reached this level. One telltale sign is when a company has an unexpected increase in acquisitions, especially large ones. This certainly increases the risks in terms of integration and execution. Plus, there could be a drain on cash because of high valuations. Next, management will begin to downplay expectations. Or, instead of focusing on revenues, they will point to profits. The company may also pursue cost-cutting measures. A company may even go into new markets to continue its growth rate. But, this is a risky thing—and gets tougher when a company is fairly large and cannot move as fast anymore.

FAILED BUSINESS MODEL

A "business model" is the way a company generates profits. But there are companies that have a failed approach or business model—and this can ultimately mean a plunge in the valuation. In some cases, it may actually be impossible to understand the business model. This is known as a "black box." This is often a red flag for short sellers. For short seller Jim Chanos, he thought Enron was a classic black box. Even after spending much time analyzing the financials, he could not understand how the company made money. Despite this, many Wall Street analysts were cheerleaders of the stock. They just assumed that management understood the company and that growth would continue.

When looking at a company's business model, a short seller will also focus on the cost structure. In some cases, a company will never make money because of the costs of delivering the product or service. Such a company was Pets.com, which was a dot-com darling. While the company sold large amounts of dog food, it could not make up for the expensive storage and shipping costs.

Interestingly enough, a business model may be viable yet it will still concern short sellers. How? This is when the market is a "niche." Even if a company makes money, the market size may not be big enough to generate enough growth for Wall Street investors. This happened with many so-called business-to-business (B2B) online companies during the 1990s. True, these companies were targeting large markets—such as chemicals. The problem was that the revenues constituted small percentages of the opportunity. Actually, as time went by, these margins got smaller and smaller.

Another red flag for short sellers is when a company periodically changes its business model. This is not to imply that change is bad. But, it does raise concerns if a company cannot seem to find a consistent way to generate profits.

DECLARING WAR ON THE SHORTS

From time to time, a company will fight the shorts. This could be with press releases or press conferences. Or, a company may pursue litigation and find ways to prevent the short selling (such as by imploring investors to take their shares out of "street name"). But such actions may really just be a way to deflect investors away from the true problems of a company. If the company is really in a good position, then the short positions will eventually drop as the stock price increases. The fact is that buyers will seek out value and growth opportunities.

Short sellers are often encouraged when they see companies fight back. Actually, a study from Owen Lamont supports this. Based on the analysis from the period of 1977 to 2002, the stock prices of such companies are usually overvalued and fall.[2]

RESIGNATIONS

Short sellers pay attention when there is a sudden resignation of the CEO or chief financial officer (CFO). This is especially the case if it is for "personal reasons" and when the company is apparently still growing. Why leave if things are good? Another telltale sign is if there is no immediate replacement for the executive. Rather, there is an interim leader. Thus, a short seller will wonder: Did the executive leave because of impending troubles? Or did the board depose him or her because of major problems?

Besides resignations, short sellers key on other issues regarding management. They will research the backgrounds, asking questions like: Are they qualified to run the company? Do they have a questionable past? Some of the red flags include personal bankruptcies, as well as regulatory sanctions.

---

[2] http://fisher.osu.edu/~diether_1/b822/overpricing.pdf.

HYPE

Public companies usually try to look at things with the "cup half full." It's inevitable—and often helpful. Management needs to be upbeat and keep moving forward. But for some companies, the enthusiasm goes too far and the messaging turns to hype. If a company's senior management spends too much time on this—such as media appearances, press releases, investor conferences, and so on—there may not be enough time to focus on the core business. In other words, an effective management team needs to be balanced. If it is not, this can be an opportunity for short sellers. For example, they will try to find situations where the stock is "priced for perfection." This is when a company is truly strong but the hype has driven the stock value to unsustainable levels. So when the company slips, the plunge in the stock price can be significant and also cause havoc on the organization.

Short sellers will also look at the "front cover" indicator. It may seem somewhat silly but it has merit. That is, beware of a company that gets a hugely positive story on the front page of a leading publication, like *BusinessWeek* or *Fortune*. It's hard to beat this kind of exposure—but it can be difficult to live up to the expectations. This is not to say that the media's coverage is off-base. If anything, it is a tremendous source of useful information. Short sellers definitely get interested when a top media outlet has a negative slant on a company. This can be a starting point to do further research.

This was the case of Jim Chanos. He learned about some of the problems at Enron from a report in the *Wall Street Journal*.

AGGRESSIVE MERGERS

Mergers are an effective way to grow and expand the depth of a company. At the same time, there are many risks. Keep in mind that a variety of academic studies show that the buyer generally overpays for a deal.

Because of this, the analysis of mergers is helpful for short sellers. To this end, they get interested when there is a transformative deal. As the name implies, a "transformative deal" is a large acquisition that fundamentally changes a company. A classic example is the AOL–Time-Warner transaction. The vision was that this merger would combine traditional media with digital pizzazz. Of course, the results were a disaster. And this was no fluke. It is common for transformative deals to not live up to lofty expectations. Perhaps the biggest reason is that it is extremely difficult to get two different cultures to integrate into one new organization.

Short sellers will look at the first-day action in the buyer's stock. Many academic studies show that investors tend to be right about their initial reaction to a deal. So if the stock price of a buyer falls more than 10 percent on the announcement of the acquisition, then the deal is likely to be problematic. Actually, short sellers will get transaction ideas by scanning for sharp drops in a company's stock price—even if there is no serious news on it. A good benchmark is a 5-percent drop. A short seller will wonder:

- Are major shareholders getting concerned?
- Are insiders dumping stock?
- Are the hedge funds getting antsy?

Keep in mind that a company's management may be tempted to hold back certain information. This may be the time to take a wait-and-see approach to see if things eventually get better (say by the end of the quarter). In the meantime, there may be steady selling.

NEXT SHOE TO DROP

If a short seller believes that a company's financials are questionable, he or she may wait until a month or so before the filing of the fourth-quarter results. Why? Bear in mind that the results from the first, second, and third quarters are unaudited results, which means it is easier for management to fudge the numbers. But the fourth-quarter results must pass muster with the auditor, which can uncover the problems.

Take John Paulson. The hedge fund investor shorted the shares of New Century in January 2007, in anticipation of the fourth-quarter numbers that would come out on February 7. He believed that the company was not fully reporting the troubles with its subprime business. And he turned out to be right. New Century reported an unexpected loss and the stock price plummeted.

FAMILY TIES

Some great companies have been family businesses. A prime example is Ford Motor Company. But for short sellers, there is often concern. If family members have several executive positions and board seats, there may be too much group-think and control. Short sellers also look for examples of "related-party transactions." This is when a company makes a deal with another entity that has substantial control from a family member. The problem here is that it is tough to get a fair deal—and shareholders may ultimately suffer.

A stark example is cable television operator, Adelphia. John Rigas founded the company in the early 1950s and led the company to tremendous growth. He also had several of his family members run key parts of the company. The problem was that there were little internal controls and the family members engaged in insider dealing, questionable loans, and the issuance of false financial statements. As the scandal came to light in 2002, the shares of Adelphia went from $30 to below $1.

FINDING A CATALYST

Short sellers will try to anticipate major events that will drive down a company's stock price. These are often referred to as "catalysts." There are several common ones that short sellers look for. One is the weather. A hurricane or major storm can have a significant impact on insurance companies, for example. For the Atlantic coast, the hurricane season lasts from June 1st until November 30th. The National Oceanic and Atmospheric Administration (NOAA) issues a hurricane outlook for each year, which has probabilities of the number and severity of the activity.

Another area that provides many catalysts is commodities. Of course, one of the most influential commodities is oil, since many businesses rely on it. For some industries, a spike in oil prices can wreak havoc on a company's financials. One example is the airline industry. It is not uncommon for airline industry shares to fall 50 percent to 60 percent when oil doubles.

STOCKS TO SHORT

Investors have a myriad ways of categorizing stocks. It's helpful when coming up with investment strategies. Although this process is usually for those who buy stocks, the same thing can be done with short-sale prospects. Here's a look.

Blue Chips

"Blue chips" are the mega-companies like Coca-Cola, IBM, and Microsoft. They have enviable products and services—which have grown despite economic instability. During bear markets, blue chips tend to perform relatively better because of the lower risk levels.

So does this mean that short sellers should avoid blue chips? Not necessarily. Interestingly enough, blue chips can be a source of short-sale targets. Keep in mind that blue chips are vulnerable to technology disruptions. Just look at companies like Kodak, which has lost a large amount of market value over the years. Short sellers also like blue chips because of the heavy trading in these stocks. This makes it easier to borrow the shares at a low cost.

Income Stocks

"Income stocks" are companies in stable industries, like utilities. Because of their strong cash flows, they generally distribute high dividends. Of course, this is a problem for short sellers since they are required to pay dividends to the party they borrowed the shares from. So for the most part, short sellers avoid income stocks.

But there are some exceptions. Some income stocks may not be generating enough cash flows to pay a dividend. Ultimately, there will need to be a cut, which can mean a plunge in the stock price.

Growth Stocks

"Growth stocks" are companies that consistently grow their sales and earnings at a rapid clip. The rates can easily be 20 percent to 30 percent per year. As a result, investors will usually put a premium valuation on growth stocks. In some cases, the P/E ratios can be substantial.

Growth stocks are fertile ground for selecting short-sale targets. But savvy short sellers will typically not take a position in a company just because it is overvalued. So long as a company continues to grow—and meet Wall Street expectations—the stock price can remain at lofty levels. Instead, a short seller will try to identify signs that the growth rates are diminishing. When this happens, growth stocks can see a substantial fall in value.

Value Stocks

"Value stocks" are companies that have already fallen in value. Reasons include that the industry is out-of-favor or that the company has experienced recent troubles. Value stocks usually have relatively low P/E ratios and the prospects for growth are minimal. The upshot is that the stock may trade in a tight range for a long time. Because of this, value stocks are usually not good short-sale prospects.

Cyclical Stocks

"Cyclical stocks" are companies that are highly sensitive to the economic cycle. That is, when the economy rebounds, there will be a surge in sales and profits. But, when the economy slips into a recession, the reverse happens. Examples of cyclical stocks include those that sell high-priced items, such as cars or homes. Commodities companies are also cyclical.

The volatility is certainly attractive to short sellers. It can be a way to make a quick profit. However, it is not necessarily easy to predict when the economy will fall into a recession.

Speculative Stocks

"Speculative stocks" are companies that are in the early stages of development. For example, they may be in biotech or alternative energy, where it may take many years for the product to get traction. This means that speculative stocks will have losses for a prolonged period of time, which usually means high levels of volatility. Again, this is attractive to short sellers. In fact, they may short speculative stocks when the valuations reach high levels.

Also, another time to short a speculative stock is when the company gets close to launching its product. It is not uncommon for there to be troubles at this point.

Penny Stocks

"Penny stocks" are shares that sell at low prices, such as below $1 per share. These companies may actually have large amounts of revenues but have suffered from hard times. But the most common types of penny stocks are those that have minimal revenues and perhaps do not even have any products. It should be no surprise that the volatility in penny stocks can be substantial.

While this should be good for short sellers, there are problems. First, penny stocks typically trade on small markets, such as the Pink Sheets or the OTC Bulletin Board. The problem here is that penny stocks have small amounts of liquidity, which increases the costs of a trade. This is because of the bid-ask spread. For the investor, the bid is what he or she can sell the stock at; the ask is the purchase price. For highly liquid stocks, the spread may be minimal, even a penny. But when it comes to penny stocks, the spread could be well over 1 percent. Another problem with penny stocks is that it can be extremely difficult to get clearance to trade them in a margin account. The result is that there may be few, if no, shares available to borrow.

As seen in this chapter, a short seller has many tools to find investment ideas. It can take lots of research but the rewards can be great—and exhilarating. In the next chapter, we will look at the core concepts of accounting and financial analysis, which are critical for success with short selling.

CHAPTER 5

Basic Accounting for Short Sellers

Key Concepts

- The federal securities laws
- The key filings like the 10-Ks and 10-Qs
- Conference calls and earnings release

While not glamorous—and often dry—a company's financial statements tell a story. And yes, some of the top short sellers have a strong grasp of the nuances. Take Jim Chanos. When evaluating a short-sale prospect, he will often spend hours combing through the financials.

Even though accounting is supposed to provide an accurate picture of a company, this is often not the case. The fact is that the U.S. accounting standards are somewhat amorphous and subject to various interpretations and assumptions. Because of this, company managements may be tempted to get aggressive with the financials. So for a savvy short seller, he or she will try to uncover these tricks.

Keep in mind that many investors simply do not dig into the financials—even those who are from top firms. One reason is the complexity. Financials involve learning new jargon and understanding how various parts of a company interrelate. Besides, the subject can be somewhat tedious and even boring. Is it any wonder that investors would rather focus on analyzing a company's cool products? There are also a large number of investors who ignore the financials because they think the best way to pick stocks is to focus on charts. The belief is that price patterns and volume levels will provide the right clues to make good investment decisions. Regardless, the fact is that many short sellers focus on financial statement analysis. Let's see how.

EMERGENCE OF THE FEDERAL SECURITIES LAWS

As the Great Depression deepened and the stock market continued to fall during the 1930s, President Franklin Delano Roosevelt and Congress realized that there needed to be significant reform for the securities industry. But regulating the securities market posed lots of challenges. If the rules were too stringent, they would continue to stifle growth and make it difficult for the economy to recover. But at the same time, if the regulations were too weak, then investors might not have enough confidence with their investment dollars.

So there were two possible options for regulation. First, the federal government could use "merit review." This means it would intensely research any proposed investment and indicate if it was worthy for the public. While this may have prevented some frauds, there were big drawbacks. For example, a merit review system would be costly and involve a massive bureaucracy. Besides, should the government really be the arbiter of what you can invest in? The next possibility was to have a regulatory system based on "disclosure." Before a company sold its securities to the public, it would need to make available the necessary documents so investors could evaluate the investment. So if the investment was shaky, this would be fine—so long as the company provided enough details. According to Supreme Court Justice Louis Brandeis, "Sunshine is said to be the best disinfectants; the electric light the most efficient policeman."[1]

After much debate, President Roosevelt and Congress agreed that the disclosure principle was the best approach. They formu-

---

[1] http://www.nysscpa.org/cpajournal/2003/1203/nv/nv2.htm.

lated this with two landmark pieces of legislation. The first was the Securities Act of 1933. The basic premise was that for any sale of securities to the public, a company would need to draft a "prospectus." This would have the financials, business plan, and risk factors. If the investor was an institution or wealthy individual, then a company might be exempted from the SEC disclosures. These exemptions are often for higher-risk investments, such as for private equity buyouts, venture capital transactions, and hedge fund investments.

Next, Congress passed the Securities Exchange Act of 1934. The focus of this legislation was on securities that were already trading in the marketplace. To this end, the 1934 Act regaled stock exchanges and brokerage firms. And over time, the mandate was broadened, such as when electronic trading platforms emerged during the 1990s. The Act also required that public companies provide ongoing disclosures to investors. What's more, it prohibited any fraudulent actions, such as misrepresentations or omissions of material information.

To enforce these regulations, the 1934 Act established the Securities and Exchange Commission (SEC), the federal agency that enforces the securities laws. The SEC's authority includes oversight of stocks, bonds, mutual funds, and even hedge funds. The SEC has five Commissioners who are appointed by the president. They make key decisions on enforcement actions and new regulatory rules. The SEC can bring civil lawsuits—but not criminal lawsuits. Instead, it is the Justice Department that can bring criminal actions for violations of federal securities laws. As such, short sellers pay close attention to the actions of the SEC. If a company is under a regulatory investigation—or must pay a fine—then there may be further problems.

Over the years, the SEC has come under more criticism, though. One of the concerns is that the agency has a tough time finding qualified regulators. After all, they will often prefer high-paying jobs on Wall Street. Next, the SEC has been under budgetary restraints. These reasons may help explain why the SEC has missed catching serious problems in the financial markets including Enron, the Indian outsourcing company Satyam, and Bernie Madoff (who engaged in a $65-billion Ponzi scheme over a 30-year period).

FINANCIAL CONTROLS

Even a small public company needs a sophisticated financial reporting infrastructure. This often involves having a computer system that handles complex accounting. It is usually the responsibility of the chief financial officer (CFO) to oversee the system and make sure that the reporting is accurate. This involves the management of different departments, as well as third parties (customers and vendors).

Because of the importance of the position, short sellers will certainly look into the background of the CFO. If he or she lacks much experience with public companies, this will definitely be a red flag. Another area a short seller will look at is the quality of a company's "internal controls." This is the overall process of how a company deals with core areas like disclosures, accounting, and so on.

Under the Sarbanes-Oxley Act, Sections 302 and 404 require that the CEO and CFO certify that the company's internal controls are accurate and meet federal standards. If there are deficiencies, the company must disclose these to shareholders (usually in the "Risk Factors" section). For a short seller, this is yet another red flag. It indicates that there is a lack of organization in a company.

MAIN TYPES OF FINANCIAL STATEMENTS

Public companies are required to make a large number of filings, which have technical names. The good news is that there are only a handful of filings that are very important for short sellers. They include the 10-Q, 10-K, annual report, proxy statement, 8-K, and insider transactions. Some of these reports come out during set times, which are based on a company's accounting period. This may be a calendar year or a fiscal year (which starts in any month other than January). For example, because of the holiday season, the fiscal year for a retailer often starts on October 1st.

What if a company is based in another country? So long as the shares trade in the United States, the company must abide by the SEC filing requirements. You can find a company's financial statements from many sources, including the SEC Web site (www.sec.gov), financial sites like Yahoo! Finance (finance.yahoo.com), and the company's own Web site (the materials will usually be in the section called "Investor Relations").

MODERN ACCOUNTING

The principles of modern accounting have been in existence since the Middle Ages. It was during this time that Luca Pacioli developed the framework known as "double-entry bookkeeping." This was a breakthrough and was critical in allowing the spread of commerce throughout Europe.

As an indication of the power of double-entry bookkeeping, it is still the bedrock of accounting today—whether a company is a corner restaurant or Wal-Mart. The premise is that every financial transaction should be recorded and balanced. For example, if a company purchases inventory, this will be recorded as an asset. But an equal amount will be deducted from the cash balance.

It's true that accounting has undergone many changes over time. But then again, the professional abides by another key principle: conservatism. Accounting rules tend to stay the same—unless there is a compelling reason to make a change. The reason is that managers and investors rely on accounting to make critical decisions. So if the rules are fluid, it could result in underperformance. Conservatism is also more than having stability in the rules. It determines the value of an asset or a liability. For example, an asset is recorded at its cost and it is not adjusted for any increase in market value. Why? Such an increase is subject to judgment and could allow managers to overstate performance. But this can sometimes result in weird things. A classic example is when a company purchased real estate decades ago. It will be recorded at its cost even though the value of the property is several times more.

Conservatism may have other unintended consequences. This happens when new innovations become an important part of Corporate America and the rules provide little guidance. Just look at the importance of derivatives or off-balance sheet liabilities. For many years, companies were able to manipulate their financial results because the rules were outmoded. Regardless of conservatism, the accounting rules still have a variety of areas that are subject to judgment. Consider pension liabilities. To estimate these, a company has no choice but to come up with a forecast of the rate of return of the assets in the trust. It should be no surprise that the temptation is to be optimistic, which lowers the company's pension liabilities.

Accounting is far from perfect and it will continue to evolve over time, especially as finance gets more complicated and companies move into foreign markets. Such things give managements opportunities to push the envelope in terms of accounting, which short sellers need to be alert to. True, using "aggressive accounting" is not necessarily bad or illegal. It's an approach where a company focuses on the many gray areas and essentially assumes the best-case scenario. However, when this is done on a consistent basis, the financials can easily get inflated. The result is that the quality of earnings is usually low.

Sometimes this leads to "fraudulent accounting." There are various forms, such as falsifying financials. This involves not including certain key items or delaying the disclosure. Again, investors could easily be misled and buy the stock.

Some managements may also engage in "self-dealing." This is when they divert corporate money to themselves or family members. Take the former CEO of Tyco, Dennis Kozlowski. State and federal authorities accused him of looting the company. Tyco paid for his multimillion-dollar Fifth Avenue apartment, which included a $6,000 shower curtain and a $38,000 backgammon table. Kozlowski said it was a necessary expense to help the company get new business. But regulators considered them to be over-the-top expenditures.

It can be tough to convict senior managers for fraudulent activities. The schemes are often complicated matters, involving thousands of pages of documents and materials. Managements will often defend their actions by saying that their advisors—such as the board, accountants, and attorneys—signed off on the activities. As a result, authorities will find novel ways to achieve their convictions. One common approach is to charge executives with "insider trading." This is when they buy or sell shares of the company stock when they have material information that has not been disclosed to the public.

Table 5-1 details the sentences of some of the most notable corporate criminals.

Besides this, fraudulent accounting can have a terrible impact on a company's shares. In some cases, bankruptcy may be the result. According to a survey from Glass Lewis & Co., there was an average 77-percent negative return for the 30 largest accounting scandals between 1997 and 2004. The shareholder destruction was about $900 billion.

Table 5-1

Some Sentences of Notable Corporate Criminals

Company	Senior Executive	Sentence
Enron	Kenneth Lay, CEO	Convicted on 25 charges, but died before sentencing
	Jeffrey Skilling, CEO	24-year sentence
	Andrew Fastow, CFO	6-year sentence; his wife served a 1-year term for signing a false tax return
WorldCom	Bernie Ebbers, CEO	25-year sentence
	Scott Sullivan, CFO	5-year sentence

ACCRUAL ACCOUNTING

Another key principle for public companies is "accrual accounting." For the most part, there are two key principles. First, *a company must record revenues when they are earned*. If a company ships a product to a customer, then there is revenue. It does not matter that cash has yet to be paid. Keep in mind, however, that this does not apply to cash-based businesses like retailers or e-commerce businesses such as Amazon.com. But these are the exceptions. It is often the case that a customer will pay within 30 to 40 days of the initial sale. Next, *a company must record its expenses when they are incurred*. Thus, if a company agrees to purchase supplies from a vendor, the expense is recognized at this point. Again, it is irrelevant if the company issues a check or not.

Why go through all this? It actually is part of another important idea in accounting: the "matching principle." In other words, companies need to find a way to match up revenues with expenses. If done solely looking at cash inflows and outflows, the results are likely to be misleading and companies may make bad decisions.

GENERALLY ACCEPTED ACCOUNTING PRINCIPLES

When reporting financials, a company must conform to "generally accepted accounting principles (GAAP)," which are a complicated array of rules, standards, and interpretations. Because of this, accountants will often specialize in a few areas of GAAP. Where do these rules come from? They are actually the contributions of a variety of organizations, such as the American Institute of Certified Accountants (AICPA), the IRS, and the SEC. However, the main source is the Financial Accounting Standards Board (FASB).

Some companies will try to avoid GAAP and instead have investors focus on "pro forma results." Needless to say, these are usually more favorable. But for short sellers, they will look past this and prefer to focus on the more conservative GAAP approach. It is tougher to manipulate things.

The GAAP approach is not the only one available. There is also the International Financial Report Standards (IFRS), which was developed by the International Accounting Standards Board (IASB). Already more than 100 countries have agreed to abide by this global standards approach. By 2011, U.S. companies will have the option of either staying with GAAP or moving over to IFRS.

The differences between the two standards are far from easy to understand. But there are some important considerations. With IFRS, the standard allows for the revaluation of assets that have increased in value over time. This goes against the conservatism principle. As can be expected, there is much debate on the topic. But if a company is asset rich, it may wind up using the IFRS standard, which could mean an immediate boost to the value of the company. At the same time, it will mean that a short seller will need to understand a new accounting standard.

AUDITS

At the end of the calendar or fiscal year, a public company must get a full-blown audit. A third-party accounting firm does this. An audit is time-consuming and expensive. A company can easily spend several million dollars on one. One reason is that an audit firm faces huge liability if the conclusions prove incorrect. Just look at Arthur Andersen. Its failed audits of Enron ultimately led to the firm's demise.

An audit is more than an analysis of financial records and reviewing GAAP policies. Rather, it involves interviews with various people within the company. It will even include discussions with vendors and suppliers. Another important part of an audit is "testing the inventory." This is actually a physical count of the inventory on hand. This is an area that is ripe for misleading reports.

To avoid problems with the process, a company will often have an internal audit team. They will ensure that the policies are in force and the accounting is proper.

Up until the passage of the Sarbanes-Oxley (SOX) Act in 2002, the audit process had some major issues. One issue was that an audit firm would also have its own consulting arm, such as for information technology (IT) integration. But this posed conflict-of-interest problems. Look at Enron. The company's accounting firm, Arthur Andersen, generated more than $50 million a year on consulting engagements while also auditing the books. In light of this, would the firm be as forceful on the audit if it might mean losing its consulting business? Because of this, Sarbanes-Oxley prohibited the consulting business for auditors.

The law has also made it more difficult to fire an auditing firm if there is a dispute. In fact, the issues must be disclosed to shareholders. Sarbanes-Oxley also created the Public Company Accounting Oversight Board (PCAOB). This organization provides independent oversight of firms providing audit services. There is also registration for auditors and periodic inspections.

Despite all this, audits are far from foolproof. For large public corporations, it's nearly impossible to investigate everything. Instead a firm will take samples and try to spot-check problems. But if an audit firm does uncover problems or even abruptly resigns, then a short seller will be alerted.

10-Q FILINGS

The "10-Q" is a comprehensive disclosure for the quarterly results of a company. It is for the first, second, and third quarters. The fourth quarter is actually included in the 10-K, which will be discussed later. In terms of the deadline, a company must release its 10-Q within 35 days of the end of the quarter.

A short seller will scrutinize the 10-Q for the trends in the financials, focusing on the income statement, balance sheet, and cash flow statement. But there are some other key parts:

- **Incorporation:** Each public company must incorporate in a state or country (which is disclosed on the first page of the 10-Q). For many public companies, the state of choice is Delaware. Short sellers get concerned if a company is incorporated in a state like Nevada or in another country such as Bermuda. The main reason is that these jurisdictions are fairly lax in terms of corporate governance.
- **Legal Proceedings:** A company will disclose any material lawsuits. While litigation is common in Corporate America, short sellers will focus on those cases that can cause serious disruption. One example is environmental exposure. Consider the litigation regarding asbestos, which resulted in the bankruptcies of various companies. Another case was the BP oil spill, which resulted in billions of dollars in liability exposure.
- **Labor Negotiations:** A short seller will follow this carefully and also do further research. If a company gets a bad settlement—or there is a strike—the impact can be severe on the stock price.
- **Defaults:** If a company is unable to pay the interest on its debt or does not comply with the terms of a loan, then there is a default. In many cases, the company will renegotiate the loan. But even if this happens, the company will likely take time to recover. In the meantime, the stock price is likely to fall, which will make for a profitable trade for short sellers.

10-K FILING

The "10-K" filing includes a comprehensive look at the financials for the whole year. A company must file this within 60 days of the end of the year. The 10-K is not to be confused with the annual report, which has fewer details and often has a flashy, glossy feel.

The following are some of the key areas that a short seller will focus on when analyzing the 10-K.

Business Summary

This is essentially a company's business plan. And despite being called a "summary," it can run on for 50 pages or more. This section will cover areas like the products and services a company offers, competition, business model, main customers, distribution system, and competitive advantages. In other words, a short seller will get a good understanding of the company. However, if it is still unclear—especially the business model—then there could be problems for the company.

Management's Discussion and Analysis

This is management's explanation of the financials. This will include discussions of industry trends, new products, the competition, and so on. Because of securities regulations, management's discussion and analysis (MD&A) must be fairly conservative. As a result, short sellers can get lots of good information from this section.

Auditor's Report

This is only a page long but it provides crucial information. The auditor's report analyzes the fairness of the financial disclosures as well as whether they are in compliance with GAAP requirements. It is not the role of the auditor's report to uncover fraud or embezzlement; however, an auditor may uncover such things and has an obligation to bring this to the attention of management—and perhaps regulators. In light of the fraud scandals over the years, auditors have boosted their fraud detection capabilities.

If an auditor finds that everything appears to be fine, then it will provide an "unqualified" or "clean" opinion. However, if there are disagreements, the report will indicate these. For example, there may be note of high-risk areas, such as related-party transactions and changes in accounting rules and methods.

Perhaps the most interesting to shareholders is a "going concern." This means that—based on the current financials—the auditor believes that the company may not have enough cash to continue to operate. Unless there is a sudden improvement in the business or an infusion of outside financing, bankruptcy is a possibility.

An auditor also has the option of giving a "qualified opinion." This means the disagreement is serious, such as involving the failure to disclose a material item. The report will provide the reasons for the disagreement. The worst type of qualified opinion from an auditor is the "adverse opinion." With this, the auditor indicates that the company is clearly providing misleading financial statements. In some cases, the auditor will disclaim the opinion and end its engagement.

THE ANNUAL REPORT

While the annual report often has lots of nonessential information—and fluff—a short seller can still find some clues about underlying problems. This usually involves getting a sense of the tone of the document. One common area for this is the "Chairman's Letter." Chances are that the Chairman did not write this! Instead, it was probably a collaboration of senior executive officers, a public relations firm, and diligent securities attorneys. It should be no surprise that this letter often puts the best face on a company. But some things may pop out. For example, some short sellers will try to look for the words "challenging," "difficulties," and "restructuring." These are often corporate-speak to hide underlying problems. It is also a good idea to read prior reports. Were these buzzwords there as well?

Finally, the Chairman's Letter will often talk about major initiatives. But does the company follow through on its promises? Again, it is helpful for short sellers to read the past five or six letters to get a feel for the overall performance of the company.

PROXY STATEMENTS

As a shareholder, you will get a "proxy statement" (this is also known as "DEF-14"). This is a disclosure document that allows for voting on key matters like new directors, the auditor, and changes in the option plan.

When reviewing the proxy, a short seller will typically look at the executive compensation section. While it is common for executives to make millions in salaries, this is usually not their main source of income. In fact, it will likely be just a small part of the compensation package. Of course, the largest component is in the form of company equity, such as restricted stock grants and options. On its face, this means that the interests between the managers and the shareholders are aligned. But this can be misleading. For example, a CEO may get a substantial amount of stock options. If the stock only increases by a small amount, the result can be millions of dollars in compensation.

Consider the survey from the *Wall Street Journal* that looked at the top 25 earners between 2000 and 2010. The top on the list was Larry Ellison, the CEO of Oracle. He received $1.84 billion in compensation. But his firm also saw its stock price triple. Then there was Apple's Steve Jobs, who earned $749 million (his salary was only $1 per year and he has not sold any shares so far). His company's shares soared 12 times.

But this does not necessarily mean that high pay means better performance. Seven of the companies actually lost money. Some notable examples include:

- **Lehman Brothers' CEO, Richard Fuld:** He earned $457 million. Of course, his company went bust.
- **Dell's CEO, Michael Dell:** He earned $454 million. His company's stock price plunged 66 percent.[2]

So a short seller will want to see a compensation package that:

- Is reasonable in terms of the number of shares
- Is based on certain milestones (say an increase in profits)
- Has a clawback if the executive departs after a short period of time

INSIDER TRANSACTIONS

Executives often buy and sell shares of their company's stock. But this raises a big issue: don't they have access to important information that could put them in an unfair position when making trades? This is certainly true. But, it would be unreasonable to deny any trading.

To deal with this problem, the federal securities laws have several regulations to help protect investors. In fact, these came

---

[2] http://online.wsj.com/article/BB1221756926688652881.html.

about because of the rampant stock manipulation during the 1920s. In order to understand the rules, it is first important to realize that they not only cover executives. Instead, they apply to a group known as "insiders." These are senior executives, corporate directors, key employees, and shareholders who own 10 percent or more of any class of the company's stock. It should be no surprise that companies try to find ways to limit the number of insiders. For example, a large company like Disney only has seven insiders. Despite this, short sellers can get useful information from the transactions of insiders.

Basically, the securities laws require that insiders need to do two main things. First, there must be disclosure of any purchase or sale of the company's securities. This is done through these filings like Form 3, Form 4, Form 5, and Form 144. Insiders must also abide by the "short-swing rule," which states that if an insider makes a profit on a transaction that has a holding period of less than six months, then the amount will be denied. This is to help encourage long-term thinking from insiders.

No doubt, the focus for short sellers is on "insider selling." And true, there are certainly many legitimate reasons for insider selling. Examples include gifts to children and relatives, diversification into other investments so as to lower the overall risk of the portfolio, contributions to charities, dividing assets for a divorce, and even paying for a large tax bill. In fact, some insiders will develop a plan where they sell a fixed amount every quarter. For the most part, this is another way for an insider to diversify his or her wealth.

So what will short sellers look for? First of all, they will focus on those insiders who likely have the most information about the company, such as the CEO and CFO. Next, short sellers will be alerted when they see "cluster selling." This is when several insiders sell large amounts of their stock at the same time. A metric would be 10 percent or more of the overall holdings. Also, has the selling been larger than in the past?

A short seller will also look at spikes in selling. If there is a small rally on the stock, are several of the insiders selling their positions? If so, it could be a sign that there is a steady attempt to bail on the stock. And, if a stock is 50 percent or more off its high and several insiders are selling off their positions—say 10 percent or more—then short sellers will certainly see this as an indication that a company is having problems. In other words, insiders have lost faith in the company's ability for a rebound and the company's problems may be severe.

EARNINGS RELEASE

When a company reports its quarterly earnings, it will put out a press release. In most cases, the tone will be optimistic. There may also be bullet points that highlight the achievements. But a short seller will dig deeper to find clues. One is the highlighting of "pro forma earnings." These are earnings that are not in compliance with GAAP. The problem is that there are no guidelines for pro forma earnings. Thus, managements can be tempted to inflate things.

For short sellers, they will certainly investigate. Are the pro forma earnings realistic? Another red flag is a missing statement. For example, the press release may not have the balance sheet or cash flow statement. Could it be that the company is trying to avoid alerting investors to problems?

CONFERENCE CALLS

After a company's earnings release, the CEO and CFO will have a conference call, which usually lasts an hour. You can access these from the company's Web site or financial portals, like Yahoo! or SeekingAlpha.com. Generally, the first 15 to 20 minutes will be an overview of the quarter. This is definitely a way to get some insight on the business and the major trends. But, it is the Question & Answer (Q&A) session with analysts that is often the most enlightening. A key thing a short seller will look for are explanations for a falloff in sales or earnings. Do the reasons make sense? Are the problems long-term? And what's the plan to deal with the problems?

Next, a short seller will want to get a sense of the "visibility." This is essentially the confidence that management has in its projections. The best gauge of this is "the guidance," which shows the quarterly and full-year forecasts. Short sellers are encouraged when there are wide ranges in these estimates. Or, in some cases, a company may even withdraw its guidance.

Another key area that short sellers will be interested in is "margins." Are they deteriorating? If so, why? A common reason is that the company is changing its product mix because it is having difficulties growing its core business. Ultimately, this could be bad news for the stock price as the business slows down and perhaps even loses money.

Short sellers will also get a feel for how management deals with analysts' questions. Are the answers evasive? Is management refusing to answer important questions? And yes, sometimes management can be hostile, which is certainly a red flag for short sellers. A famous example was Enron's conference call in 2001. In it, CEO Jeffrey Skilling called an analyst an "asshole." Within a few months, Enron was in shambles.

In this chapter, it is made apparent that seemingly accurate things like accounting and company disclosures are full of nuances and even inaccuracies. It takes practice to catch these, but it is what a good short seller does. In the next chapter, we will look at the nuts-and-bolts of the balance sheet, which shows a company's assets, liabilities, and capital position.

CHAPTER 6

Analyzing the
Balance Sheet

Key Concepts

- Types of balance sheets
- Liquidity and debt ratios
- Off-balance sheet items

A "balance sheet" shows the values of a company's assets, liabilities, and equity at a certain period of time. As the name implies, the balance sheet will balance. This is according to the following equation:

$$Assets = Liabilities + Equity$$

How can this equation always be equal? The reason is double-entry accounting. Every transaction has two equal sides. As for the balance sheet equation, it shows that a company's assets come from a combination of borrowings, as well as raising money from investors. But there is another important source: profits. For a short seller, he or she will look at whether a company needs to borrow more money because profits are declining or have gone negative. Of course, this cannot last forever and eventually the company's assets will contract, resulting in a lower stock value.

BALANCE SHEET REPORTS

Through public filings, companies will show two to five years of balance sheet reports to give investors a sense of the trends over time, and it is not uncommon for companies to have assets, liabilities, and equity that amount to millions or billions of dollars. If the full numbers were placed on the balance sheet—or any other financial statement—it would be tough to interpret. To deal with this, companies will "truncate" the numbers. One common approach is to convert the figures into thousands or even millions. Say, for example, that XYZ Corp. has $1,100,509,000 in assets. To express this in millions, it would be $1,101. As you can see, the last digit is rounded up.

There are two main types of balance sheet approaches that companies employ: the account format and the report format. Both have the same types of information but the presentation is different. With the "account format," the assets are on the left side and the liabilities and the equity are on the right side. As for the "report format," the balance sheet lists the assets, the liabilities, and then the equity. Table 6-1 shows the balance sheets for Blockbuster Video (the numbers are in millions).

First of all, note that when a figure is surrounded by parentheses, this means it is a negative number. Also, some items are not clear-cut. For example, what is the difference between merchandise inventories and the film library? To get more details, the balance sheet will have footnotes. These are required by GAAP standards. Ironically enough, however, the footnotes may also be tough to understand because of complex jargon and accounting concepts. Short sellers will spend lots of time trying to understand these footnotes as they can help uncover problems for a company.

One key area that footnotes cover is debt. What are the interest rates? When will certain debts come due? This can give a clue as to whether a company will need to raise money to cover its upcoming obligations. There will even be disclosures of "off-balance sheet obligations." These would include capital leases and pension obligations. No doubt, these can be a drain on future cash flows. Another set of important footnotes include accounting policies. Here, you will see how a company recognizes revenues and expenses. There will also be a look at the types of assumptions the

TABLE 6-1

Blockbuster Balance Sheet*

Assets	January 3, 2010	January 4, 2009
Current Assets:		
Cash and cash equivalents	$188.7	$154.9
Receivables, less allowances	79.4	117.1
Merchandise inventories	298.5	432.8
Rental library, net	298.5	432.8
Deferred income taxes	13.6	13.4
Prepaid and other current assets	139.1	184.6
Total Current Assets	**1,060.0**	**1,258.6**
Property and equipment, net	249.4	406.0
Deferred income taxes	114.6	124.3
Intangibles, net	7.7	11.5
Goodwill	0	338.1
Restricted cash	48.1	16.0
Other assets	48.1	16.0
Total Assets	**1,538.3**	**2,154.5**
Liabilities and Stockholders' Equity		
Current Liabilities:		
Accounts payable	300.8	427.3
Accrued expenses	407.7	493.8
Current portion of long-term debt	101.6	198.0
Current portion of capital lease obligations	6.1	8.5
Deferred income taxes	118.6	125.8
Total Current Liabilities	**934.8**	**1,253.4**
Stockholders' Equity:		
Preferred stock	145.9	150.0
Class A common	1.3	1.2
Class B common	0.7	0.7
Additional paid-in capital	5,377.0	5,378.4
Accumulated deficit	(5,786.9)	(5,228.7)
Accumulated other comprehensive loss	(52.3)	(87.3)
Total Stockholders' Equity	**(314.3)**	**214.3**
Total	**1,538.3**	**2,154.5**

*http://www.sec.gov/Archives/edgar/data/1085734/000119312510058339/d10k.htm

company has made, such as for depreciation expenses or the loss estimates on accounts receivables. Finally, a short seller will also find footnotes about stock options. As the stock price goes up, these options will likely be exercised, resulting in more shares of the company's stock on the market.

CASH

It's an overused phrase but it is still something that all short sellers understand: "Cash is king." Without sufficient cash on hand, even a good company can fall to pieces. This certainly was the case with Blockbuster Video. When reading the footnotes, there were several sections that analyzed the "liquidity" of the company. This included efforts to reduce costs through layoffs, store closures, lease renegotiations, and operational efficiencies.

Cash is the first item on the balance sheet. It is not just money in the bank but also cash equivalents, which include highly liquid securities like Treasuries. Some investors will even include other types of assets like accounts receivables and inventory. Short sellers, however, will ignore these types of illiquid assets. They will also ignore "restricted cash." This is cash that is for particular purposes, such as a major customer account. As a result, this should be excluded from a company's cash balance since it is not really liquid.

Next, a short seller will look for quarterly deterioration in the cash balance. Is it falling even though earnings are increasing? Yes, this seems strange but it is common for weak companies. Keep in mind that management can get aggressive in how it reports earnings, but it can do very little in terms of showing more cash on the balance sheet.

Another helpful metric for short sellers is "cash per share," which they will look at in an attempt to identify quarter-to-quarter trends. To calculate this, you can use the following formula:

(Cash + Marketable Securities) / Shares Outstanding

A short seller will also calculate the "burn rate." To do this, you will find the average quarterly reduction in the cash balance and assume this continues. How long will it take for the company to run out of cash? If a company is on track to evaporate its cash within two years, this is an alert to a short seller. Either the company will need to aggressively cut back on expenses or raise more capital, which can dilute existing shareholders.

ACCOUNTS RECEIVABLES

Accounts receivables include the amount of money that customers owe a company. In a sense, this is credit that has been extended to customers. While there is nothing necessarily bad about accounts receivables, short sellers will often spend much analysis on it. One reason is that it reduces cash flows. For example, suppose a company generates $50 million in sales but it takes six weeks to collect the cash from customers. This means that—on average—the following will be accounts receivables:

$$(6 \text{ weeks} / 52) \times \$50 \text{ million} = \$5.7 \text{ million}$$

But suppose that it takes only four weeks to collect the receivables. The result would be that the amount would fall to $3.8 million. In other words, a company would have an additional $1.9 million in cash on average.

There are helpful tools that short sellers will use to analyze accounts receivables. One is looking at the allowance for doubtful accounts. This is also known as an "accrual," which means that management has discretion in terms of coming up with an estimate. Needless to say, this can lead to inflated earnings. As for the "allowance for doubtful accounts," this is the estimated percentage of accounts receivables that are likely not to be collected. This is subtracted from the accounts receivables. A low-ball amount will boost receivables as well as profits. Short sellers will be skeptical when they see that the estimate is significantly lower than the industry benchmarks or it is decreasing while accounts receivables are increasing. Another danger sign is when there is a major drop in the percentage.

The "allowance for doubtful accounts" is similar to the concept of "loan-loss reserves" for financial institutions. This is an estimate that the loan assets will need to be charged off. For example, from 2001 to 2007, U.S. banks were actually reducing their loan-loss reserves. The belief was that the economy would continue to grow and asset values would remain strong. But of course, this proved to be a disaster as the financial system nearly collapsed. The loan-loss reserves greatly underestimated the bad debts. The upshot was a spike in losses, which required the federal government to engage in a massive bailout.

To gauge accounts receivables, short sellers will also analyze the "days sales outstanding (DSO)." It shows how many days it takes to convert accounts receivables into cash. Here's the calculation:

(Ending Receivables / Credit Revenue) × Number of Days in the Period[1]

There are variations on this calculation but the above is a good approximation. And yes, companies may have their own approach, which will likely make things better than they seem.

What is a good DSO? It really depends on the industry. So it is a good idea to compute this for rivals. If you see that a company has a number that is 30 days or higher than the average, this could be a sign that a company is being aggressive with its accounting or is having problems collecting from customers.

Short sellers will also look to see if there is a disconnect between a company's sales and its accounts receivables. True, there will likely to be differences in the growth rates of sales and accounts receivables. However, a short seller will look for major discrepancies. This would be the case if sales increased 50 percent but accounts receivables spiked by 100 percent. This may be an indication of bad earnings quality. One reason would be that a company is loosening its credit standards so as to pump up sales. Or, there may be bad collection policies or aggressive sales approaches, such as "stuffing the channel." This means shipping more products to customers than has been requested.

INVENTORY

There are three kinds of inventory. First, there are "raw materials," which are the basic components to build a product. Examples include steel and plastic. Next, there is "work-in-progress." These are the items that have yet to be finished. Finally, a company will

---

[1] There are usually 91.25 days in a typical quarter.

have "finished goods." As the name implies, this is when an item is ready to ship to customers.

Inventory is a critical component for a company's gross profits but is subject to manipulation from management. To understand this, let's take an example:

TABLE 6-2

Inventory Results Manipulation

Items	Last Year (in Millions)	Current Year (in Millions)
Sales	$100	$120
Beginning Inventory	$20	$10
Plus purchases	$30	$50
Goods for sale	$50	$60
Less ending inventory	$10	$15
Cost of goods sold	$40	$45
Gross profit	$60	$75

A company's "gross profit" is the difference between sales and the cost of goods sold (COGS). To find COGS, you need to add the inventory for the beginning of an accounting period and then add any additional inventory purchases. Then you subtract the inventory that is on hand at the end of the accounting period.

Looking at Table 6-2, last year's COGS calculation first involved adding the beginning inventory of $20 million to the additional purchases of $30 million. Then the $10 million in ending inventory was subtracted, which meant the COGS was $40 million. All this sounds good, right? The problem is for the current year. Looking at the chart, last year's ending inventory is now this year's beginning inventory, which is only $10 million. By lowering inventory costs, it is possible to create future periods of higher gross margins and ultimately, net profits. As a result, short sellers will look at a company's financial statements to see if there has been a change in the accounting for inventory. If so, there may be inflated results.

For example, a short seller would be alerted if a company changed its accounting valuation method from FIFO (First In, First Out) to LIFO (Last In, First Out). Basically, if inventory costs are rising and a company wants to understate this, it can move toward FIFO. This means that the first items purchased will be the first ones included in determining the value of inventory.

OTHER INVENTORY PROBLEMS

There are certain industries that are highly impacted by inventory. One is retail, especially those companies that focus on toys or the latest fashions. A change in consumer tastes can easily result in a pileup of useless inventory and losses for shareholders. Another vulnerable industry is technology, as consumers want to obtain the latest gadgets. But what if a new one is a dud? It can be devastating.

For short sellers, there are some areas they will look for when analyzing inventory. For example, discounts and write-offs are major red flags. Such things indicate that a company is having trouble moving inventory and is taking steps to deal with the problem. Eventually, there should be a hit to profits. Next, a short seller will look at the inventory turnover ratio. The reason is that it gives an idea about the costs of inventory, which can be quite expensive. After all, there is a need to buy and store materials for the finished goods. The longer inventory stays in a warehouse or on the store shelves, the higher the overall costs.

The "inventory turnover ratio" is:

Cost of Goods Sold / Average Inventory

A short seller will compare this to industry benchmarks, as well as see if the ratio increases over time.

Another useful inventory indicator is the "days sales of inventory (DSI)." The DSI measures the average length that inventory sits in the warehouse. If this is rising over time—and is 20 percent or longer than industry peers—then inventory could be an issue.

This is the formula:

Ending Inventory / COGS × Days in the Period[2]

---

[2] Remember, there are 91.25 days in a typical quarter.

Short sellers will also see if there are growth trends in raw materials. If these are growing faster than finished goods, then the company may be having problems with its manufacturing process. What's more, short sellers will compare inventory growth to sales. Is it moving faster? If so, this is an indication that there is lagging demand from customers. But a short seller needs to be cautious. Sometimes a company will boost inventory in anticipation of a new product launch or the holiday season.

SOFT ASSETS

Soft assets are somewhat vague and are not part of the typical classifications on a company's balance sheet. In fact, such an item may be something like "Other Assets," "Prepaid Expenses," "Other Noncurrent Assets," or even "Software Development Costs." Because of this, a short seller will read the footnotes in the financials to get a better understanding of the nature of these assets. As should be no surprise, this may reveal that a company is trying to hide certain transactions to make the financials look better. For example, a soft asset may be a way for a company to make current expenses into assets. This is known as "capitalizing expenses."

As an example, suppose XYZ Corp. is investing $5 million in an aggressive marketing campaign. No doubt, the benefits of this should last several years. So why not expense the $5 million over, say, five years? This means that in year one, a company will put $4 million as an asset and take a $1 million expense. Clearly, this will tend to overstate profits. While this may not necessarily be wrong or illegal, it does raise a red flag. This is especially the case if soft assets are increasing at a high rate, say 20 percent to 30 percent more than sales.

GOODWILL

"Goodwill" is an asset that results from acquisitions. It is the difference between the purchase price and the value of the net assets of the target company. To understand this concept, let's take an example. Suppose IBM buys XYZ Corp. for $10 million. The company develops software and has assets that amount to only $1 million. But IBM has to account for the remaining value of $9 million, which is goodwill. Think of this as an "intangible asset," which represents the value of the intellectual property, brand, and customer list. But what if the value of the goodwill is overstated? Perhaps XYZ Corp. cannot sustain its growth or keep up with the competition. To deal with this, there must be an annual goodwill check. If there is a reduction in value—called an "impairment"—a company must take a charge against earnings.

For short sellers, they will look at companies that have large amounts of goodwill on the balance sheet. If the acquisitions look too aggressive, then there may ultimately be losses in the future.

LONG-TERM ASSETS

"Long-term assets" include things like plant and equipment. Initially, a company will record these assets on the balance sheet at the original cost. But over time, the company will expense them because of wear-and-tear and obsolescence. This is known as "depreciation." Depending on the class of the asset, the term of the depreciation can vary. For example, a computer will typically have a depreciation period of five years. But a building, on the other hand, could have a term of over 30 years.

Next, a company has discretion on the type of depreciation to use. These include two main categories. First, there is "straight-line depreciation." This means that depreciation is in equal amounts for the term. So if a computer costs $2,000 and the term is five years, then the annual depreciation amount is $400. Next, a company can use "accelerated depreciation." Under this approach, a company will take a larger expense during the first or second year in the asset's life. The main reason for this is to get a higher tax deduction.

Depreciation can get highly complicated and companies like to hide this in footnotes of the financials. However, short sellers will dig in and look for red flags. First of all, it is ominous if a company lengthens the term of depreciation. This will lower the annual amount. What's more, a short seller will be alerted if there is a change in the depreciation method, for example, going from accelerated depreciation to straight-line. This will probably help to artificially boost profits.

LIABILITIES

When looking at the balance sheet, a short seller will spend lots of time scrutinizing the liabilities. These can wreak havoc on a company, especially if revenues and cash flows decline.

A company will have two types of liabilities. First, there are "current liabilities," which generally must be paid off within a year. These include:

- **Accounts Payables:** The amounts owed to vendors, such as for inventory and supplies.
- **Interest Payable:** The amount of interest expenses owed.
- **Unearned Revenues:** These are revenues received but the company has yet to deliver services or a product. For example, a customer may pay for two years' of a service. A company must account for the future revenues as liabilities.
- **Taxes:** A company is required to pay taxes on a quarterly basis.
- **Current Portion of Long-Term Liabilities:** This is when long-term debt— principal and interest—come due within the year.

The next type is "long-term debt." These are liabilities that will be paid off beyond a year. These include:

- **Bond:** A debt issued to the public. The maturity often ranges from 10 to 20 years.
- **Note:** A debt with a maturity between one to ten years.
- **Mortgage:** A loan for a building.

Of course, if a company is unable to pay its debts, then bankruptcy is likely to be the result. In this case, the stock price may be reduced to pennies—providing short sellers with the ultimate trade.

Companies have two approaches in dealing with a bankruptcy. The most common form is a "Chapter 11 bankruptcy." This is when a company has a healthy business but it cannot deal with the debt structure. So it will restructure operations and attempt to put the things on the right footing. In fact, the process has worked quite well for many companies. Next, a company may file for a

"Chapter 7 bankruptcy." This is when the business model has failed and there will be a liquidation of assets. Under this scenario, there is little value left.

Regardless of the filing, there is something that usually happens: shareholders lose much or all of their investment. The main reason is the concept of "priority of claims." That is, when a company enters bankruptcy, the debt holders get first claims on the assets. In most cases, this leaves little to nothing left for shareholders.

LIQUIDITY RATIOS

There are some common financial ratios that can give a sense of a company's liquidity. Of course, if these are weak—and deteriorating—a short seller will definitely get interested. For example, there is the "Current Ratio," which is calculated as follows:

Current Assets / Current Liabilities

A ratio of 2:1 is generally considered fairly safe, but be forewarned that there may be differences from industry to industry. After all, a major company may not need a high ratio since it has a stable business and ready access to capital.

Then there is the Quick Ratio. Some current assets may not necessarily be liquid, such as inventory. In this case, the "Quick Ratio" will be more restrictive:

(Current Assets – Inventory) / Current Liabilities

If the ratio is below 1.0, there could be potential troubles for a company.

DEBT RATIOS

There are a variety of ways to measure a company's levels of debt. One of the most common is the "debt-to-equity ratio," which is measured as follows:

Total Debt / Total Equity

A short seller will include both short-term and long-term debt in the calculation, to be as inclusive as possible. For the most part, if a company has a debt-to-equity ratio of more than 70 percent, the balance sheet has a high amount of leverage. If there are troubles with cash flow, it could be difficult to meet the company's obligations. The high leverage also makes it difficult to get more financing from lenders, which could stunt growth.

Another helpful indicator is the "times interest earned ratio." It gives a sense of a company's ability to pay its debts. Here's the formula:

Earnings Before Interest and Taxes (EBIT) / Interest Expense

EBIT is one way to calculate a company's cash flow. More importantly, lenders will often use this when making loans and setting terms. For example, a bank may require that a company maintain a times interest earned ratio of 7 or more. This provides a margin of safety for the loan. If the ratio falls below the specified level, the company will be in default and the bank has the right to require the repayment of the loan. A short seller will find these loan terms and track them over time. If a company is getting close to violating them, it could be a good indication to take a short position.

BOND PRICES

In the stock market, there are many individual investors. In some cases, they may not have lots of investment experience and as a result, buy or hold onto a stock that has major problems. The upshot is that a stock price can remain at overvalued levels—at least for a short period of time. The bond market, on the other hand, is mostly made up of institutional investors. No doubt, they are much more aware of company-specific problems and trade accordingly. As such, short sellers will often analyze bond prices of companies to gauge the overall sentiment. If it is negative, then there may be a delayed impact on the stock price.

With many online financial sites, it is much easier to research bond prices nowadays. These are quoted on a percentage of a $1,000 face value (this is the amount of money an investor gets back when the company pays back the debt). For example, suppose XYZ

Corp. has $100 million in bonds that come due in ten years. On the market, they are selling for 62.75. To translate this, you will perform the following calculation:

$$62.75\% \times \$1{,}000 = \$627.5$$

The price of a bond moves based on several key factors. One is the movement in interest rates. If interest rates increase, the price of bonds will generally decline and vice versa. The reason is that in order to remain competitive—in terms of its yield—a bond will need to adjust. So a short seller will need to account for this movement. But a bond price may also change based on company risk. If the belief is that the company will have troubles paying its debt, the price will fall.

Table 6-3 lists some guidelines on bond pricing.

TABLE 6-3

Guidelines on Bond Pricing

Prices	Explanation
80–90	There may be some problems (especially for bonds below 90). But it could be a false alarm.
60–80	Bond holders are definitely concerned and there are major doubts about a company's ability to pay its debt.
40–60	The company has probably already defaulted and bankruptcy is a likely possibility.
40 and lower	The company is probably already bankrupt.

THE Z-SCORE

There is an indicator that attempts to provide the likelihood of a corporate bankruptcy. It is called the z-score. The person who developed this indicator is Edward Altman, who won the Nobel Prize for Economics. The formula for the "z-score" is:

$$Z\text{-}Score = 1.2a + 1.4b + 3.3c + 0.6d + 1.0e, \text{ where}$$
a = working capital / total assets
b = retained earnings / total assets

c = earnings before interest and taxes (EBIT) / total assets

d = equity market capitalization / total assets

e = annual sales / total assets

As you can see, this uses a variety of important financial items from the income statement and the balance sheet—which are in reference to the total assets. Generally, the higher the z-score, the better a company's financial health. But if the z-score hits 1.8 or lower, then the company is in trouble and there may be a short-sale opportunity.

CREDIT LINES

A "credit line" is a fixed amount of financing for a company. It is available any time for a company to access it. However, in some cases, a company will unexpectedly draw on most or all of the line. True, there may be a reasonable explanation for this—such as a need to gear up for a new product or for the holiday season. But if a company is already showing signs of trouble, then a credit-line drawdown could be a red flag. Another sign is if a third-party credit agency, such as Standard & Poor's or Moody's, decided to downgrade the company's bonds.

SPECIAL LIABILITIES

Companies can get quite creative in hiding or obscuring liabilities. But of course, short sellers will try to uncover these. In fact, these kinds of liabilities can be substantial and create lots of risk for a company.

One example is a corporate pension. Even though this type of retirement benefit is rarely provided anymore, there are many companies with legacy pension liabilities. Often these are old-line companies, such as auto manufacturers and mining operators. By definition, a "pension" is a trust that invests money on behalf of its beneficiaries. The problem is that it can be difficult to get strong returns to pay off the future liabilities, especially as people live longer. To get a sense of the extent of the liability, a company will actually need to estimate the average return. Needless to say, this is subject to much discretion and can distort the results. A short seller will get concerned if a company increases the average return—which will understate the overall pension liability. This is especially the case if others in the industry have not done so and financial markets have lagged over the years.

Another area with potential red flags is a company's "off-balance sheet liabilities." As the name implies, these are liabilities that you will not find on a company's main balance sheet. Rather, you will need to search through the footnotes, which can be a tricky process. An off-balance sheet liability will often be in the form of a new venture known as a "special purpose entity (SPE)." In a sense, an SPE is a separate company, which can generate business but also keep the debt on its own balance sheet. By way of example, Enron was a notorious abuser of off-balance sheet liabilities. Interestingly enough, a variety of major financial institutions also used billions of dollars of these vehicles, which became a massive problem during the financial meltdown of 2007 to 2008.

Some short sellers have a special ratio to measure the true amount of debt:

$$(Balance\ Sheet\ Debt\ +\ Off\text{-}Balance\ Sheet\ Debt)\ /\ Equity$$

A short seller will look at the growth of this ratio over time, as well as comparisons to industry peers. In some cases, a company may use an aggressive way to account for liabilities, for example, the equity method, which can hide major assets that are usually poor segments of the business. The equity method is often for purchases of other companies. So long as the equity is less than 20 percent, a company can do a neat trick. That is, it can include the purchase as an asset on its own balance sheet but not have to report the liabilities! Because of this, short sellers consider the equity method to be an aggressive accounting method.

Or, consider leases. While this is certainly a legitimate way to grow operations, there are also opportunities for clever accounting. This depends on the type of the lease. With a "capital lease," a company will account for this as a liability on the balance sheet, which allows for a more conservative approach for disclosure. Then there is the "operating lease." With such an arrangement, a company must return the asset after the lease period. Because of this, there is no requirement to account for it on the balance sheet. So a short seller will read the footnotes to estimate the amounts of the operating leases. Then, he or she will compare this to overall sales. If it is a substantial amount, then the company is likely being aggressive with its accounting.

Finally, another area of focus for a short seller is "warranties." This is a potential liability. If a product has a problem, the company will fix it. But since it is not certain what the overall liability will be, management will need to make an estimate (this comes under the category of an accrual). The temptation is to provide a low estimate of this potential liability, which means a lower hit to earnings. Actually, this is what Dell did with its computer systems. But eventually the company had to reverse its policy and get more conservative on its estimates. You will typically find these accruals in soft accounts with names like "accrued expenses" or "other current liabilities." Short sellers will take note when there is a sudden increase in these kinds of accounts.

EQUITY

The equity part of the balance sheet shows the amount of money investors have contributed to the company, as well as the accumulated earnings and losses. If the equity part is declining, it is certainly a red flag for investors.

Typically, the largest part of the equity section is for the "common stock." This includes all the shares that a company has issued to the public. However, the price is at "par value," which is an artificial figure. In most cases, this is lower than the actual stock price the stock was issued at. To make up for this, the balance sheet will have an account called "additional paid-in capital." This represents the amount over the par value a company has issued for its common stock. Then, the balance sheet will show the Treasury stock, which includes the common shares the company has bought back.

The last item is "retained earnings." If a company has a profit, then it is added here. In other words, profits increase shareholders' equity. If there is a loss, then the reverse is true. The retained earnings are also reduced by any dividends paid. Short sellers will look at retained earnings to get a sense of the company's overall progress. If a company has a large—and growing—negative retained earnings, then it is definitely a warning sign.

EQUITY VERSUS REAL VALUE

Keep in mind that the equity value on a balance sheet is not the same as the company's market value. If anything, the market value is usually much higher.

Table 6-4 lists some examples.

TABLE 6-4

Market Value and Equity Value of Select Companies Compared

Company	Market Cap	Stockholders' Equity
Google	$156B	$36B
Ford	$43B	–$8B
Coca-Cola	$126B	$24B
IBM	$161B	$22B
Exxon	$280B	$110B

There are many reasons for the differences. For example, the equity account is based on conservative accounting valuation approaches. What's more, a company may have sustained major losses in the past or pays high dividends. Despite all this, the equity account is still worth looking at. In a way, it's a way to reflect the value of a company that is adjusted for its debt load. What's more, a short seller will often look at the "return on equity (ROE)." This is as follows:

Net Income / Equity

A short seller wants to find companies whose growth rates are higher than the ROE. The reason is that there is not enough cash flow to finance the growth. So a company will need to seek more financing, such as by issuing stock.

This raises the problem of "dilution." This is when current shareholders experience a reduction in the value of their holdings because the company has issued more shares. In some cases, this can be severe. Consider "toxic financings." Yes, this is the official name—and it's something that short sellers love to see! Toxic financings are usually seen during times when the economy is slowing and companies are having much difficulty finding capital. All in all, the cost of capital can skyrocket and ultimately result in a major reduction in the stock price.

The general structure of a toxic financing is a PIPE (private investment in public equity). True, a PIPE is not necessarily a bad thing. But if structured aggressively, it can be particularly toxic to existing shareholders.

To understand this, let's take a look at how a PIPE works. A "PIPE" is an issuance of securities through a process known as a "private placement." In this scenario, there may be only a few investors involved in the funding. Because these investors are sophisticated institutions, the disclosure requirements are not as onerous as those for public offerings. This makes the process quicker and even cheaper.

Before making an investment, the investors will usually conduct extensive "due diligence." This means that the firm has access to critical information and can get a clear sense of the status of the company. And, if things are looking bleak, investors will certainly structure a PIPE that has stringent requirements. The company will issue a "press release," which is a general description of the transaction. But a short seller will instead look at the "8-K," which provides extensive information on the terms. Short sellers specifically look at warrant coverage on the 8-K. Basically, a "warrant" gives a PIPE investor the right to buy more shares in the firm. This is called an "equity kicker." With this, the PIPE investor will get extra return on investment. But at the same time, there will be dilution for existing shareholders. Next, the PIPE investor will likely get a "convertible security." This is essentially a bond or preferred stock that allows the PIPE investor to exchange it for a certain number of shares of common stock in a company.

To provide protection, the investor will have a "reset feature." This means that the further the stock declines, the more shares the investor can convert. This can cause a so-called "death spiral," which can crater the stock. In the end, the PIPE investor will wind up owning a substantial amount of the company's stock. There may be even more benefits, such as a "liquidation preference." This means that the PIPE investor will get priority in the event of liquidation. This will usually wipe out the common shareholders. Or, there may be a "participation right" to the security. This is triggered when a company is sold. In this scenario, the PIPE investor will get the original investment back, plus any unpaid dividends, as well as the return on the investment. This will pose considerable dilution for current stockholders.

If a PIPE has some or all of the above features, the impact can be severe for current stockholders. Look at a study from professors at the Darden Graduate School of Business Administration and Pennsylvania State University. Based on their research, they found that toxic PIPEs resulted in average negative returns of 22 percent within a year of the financing.[3]

COMMON-SIZE FINANCIALS

Finding adverse trends in financial statements can be difficult. So to help things out, short sellers will create common-size income statements and balance sheets. This can be done using a spreadsheet. First, the short seller will compare at least two accounting periods—say this year versus the prior year's results. Next, he or she will use a frame of reference. For an income statement, this means that all items will be a percentage of revenues. As for the balance sheet, the reference point can be total assets.

Table 6-5 shows an example.

By looking at Table 6-5, the percentage changes provide helpful insights. Over the past year, the accounts receivables went from 4 percent of total assets to 7 percent of total assets. This may mean that the company is having trouble selling its goods. In fact, as seen with the retained earnings, the company is sustaining losses and is using some debt to pay for things. Also, there was a jump in goodwill. This could have been the result of an acquisition.

The analysis in this chapter can be daunting. Even top-notch investors do not have a good grasp of financial statement analysis. Yet to be a good short seller, it is critically important. Of course, this is also the case for investors considering a long position. The key to getting better at financial analysis is to get in the habit

---

[3] http://faculty.darden.virginia.edu/chaplinskys/documents/pipes_may%2005
.pdf.

TABLE 6-5

Balance Sheet Reference Points

	2010 (in millions)	Percentage of 2010 Revenue	2011 (in millions)	Percentage of 2011 Revenue
Cash	$10	1%	$11	1%
Net Receivables	$30	4%	$70	7%
Inventory	$50	7%	$75	7%
Total Current Assets	**$90**	**13%**	**$156**	**15%**
Plant and Equipment	$300	44%	$310	30%
Goodwill	$200	29%	$400	39%
Total Assets	**$680**	**100%**	**$1,022**	**100%**
Accounts Payables	$40	6%	$16	2%
Taxes	$15	2%	$20	2%
Long-Term Debt	$500	74%	$600	59%
Total Liabilities	**$555**	**82%**	**$900**	**88%**
Common Stock	$100	15%	$100	10%
Additional Paid-In Capital	$50	7%	$50	5%
Retained Earnings	$(25)	–4%	$(28)	–3%
Total Equity and Liabilities	**$680**	**100%**	**$1,022**	**100%**

of reading the quarterly statements. Over time, the analysis will become second nature.

In the next chapter, we will take a look at the income statement, which shows the profitability of a company. It is something that management has lots of discretion to inflate results. Thus, for a short seller, it is a source for finding investment ideas.

The Income Statement

Key Concepts

- Types of income statements
- Operating versus non-operating revenues
- Revenue recognition policies
- Analyzing earnings estimates

On Wall Street, the income statement is the most widely followed statement. Investors want to see a company continue to grow its earnings, which will lead to a higher stock price.

For several weeks after each calendar quarter, there is an "earnings season." This is when most public companies report their financials. Ahead of this, investors and analysts will try to estimate the earnings, which are generally on the mark (at least during normal times). But some companies will "surprise" investors. When this is below the expectations figure, the impact can be severe. It is not uncommon for a stock to drop 10 percent to 20 percent on such news.

INCOME STATEMENT FORMATS

On its face, the income statement is straightforward. It shows revenues and costs—with the difference being the profit or loss. Of course, there can be much complexity with these items, in terms of assumptions, accounting policies, and in some cases, even fraud. Regardless of the name, an income statement is for a period of time, such as a quarter or one year. There are also two formats—the single-step format and the multi-step format.

First, there is the "single-step format." This is the simplest approach, which has two groups—revenues and expenses. Table 7-1 shows an example.

TABLE 7-1

Sample Single-Step Income Statement

Types of Revenues and Gains	Amount
Revenues	$120,000
Interest Income	$100
Gain from Asset Sales	$20,000
Total Revenues and Gains	**$140,100**
Cost of Goods Sold	$56,040
Selling, General, and Administrative	$42,030
Interest Expense	$2,000
Depreciation	$14,010
Taxes	$5,000
Net Income	**$21,020**

Next, there is the multi-step format. This is the preferred approach, since this income statement has subtotals that allow for better analysis—such as gross profit, operating expenses, and so on. Table 7-2 provides an example.

REVENUES

"Revenues" are what a company gets from its customers for selling goods or providing services. Another term for revenues is the "top line"—since *revenues* is listed at the beginning of the income statement.

Some companies may not even have revenues. This was the case, for example, during the dot-com boom. Even today there are a variety of biotech companies that have a $0 on the top line. Yet

TABLE 7-2

Sample Multi-Step Income Statement

Types of Revenues and Gains	Amounts
Revenues	$120,000
Cost of Goods Sold	$48,000
Gross Profit	$72,000
Operating Expenses	
Selling, General, and Administrative	$36,000
Research and Development	$5,000
Operating Income	$41,000
Other Income	
Interest Income	$1,000
Gains from Asset Sales	$20,000
Other Expenses	
Interest Expense	$3,000
Depreciation	$7,000
Income Before Taxes	$52,000
Income Taxes	$8,000
Net Income	**$44,000**

they can still have valuations of hundreds of millions or billions of dollars. The belief is that the company will eventually produce a high-selling drug, which will translate into substantial revenues and profits. In other words, a company ultimately will need a strong revenue base—or the expectation of one—if it wants to be a solid public company.

OPERATING VERSUS NON-OPERATING REVENUES

"Operating revenues" are those that come from the core business of the firm. For example, in the case of Google, its operating revenue is advertising fees. These actually account for about 99 percent of the overall revenues. But a company may also have "non-operating revenues." These are from nonmaterial parts of the business or from special transactions, such as the sale of a division.

It is common for companies to have several segments for operating revenues, especially for conglomerates like GE. But there is typically one category that dominates, usually representing more than a majority of the revenue base. Short sellers will focus on this. So if the main business is seeing a slowdown in its core business, there could be troubles ahead. After all, it will probably be tough for the other parts of the company's business to make up for the shortfall.

REVENUE RECOGNITION

GAAP standards provide companies with various options in terms of revenue recognition. These often include guidance on the timing of revenues, as well as the amounts to include. Some are conservative while others are more liberal, which tend to boost revenues (at least in the short run). No doubt, a short seller will scrutinize the liberal ones. One example is the "completed contract method." This is a revenue recognition policy for companies that have long-term contracts, such as technology service providers, consulting firms, and construction operators.

A customer will typically make a partial upfront payment and then ongoing payments for milestones and requirements. So should all these payments be recognized when the contract is signed? Well, the proper approach is to recognize the revenues as the various parts of the contract are performed. The problem is that this involves estimates of performance. As a result, some companies will get aggressive and recognize a large amount of revenues upfront. In fact, there are cases like Computer Associates, which accounted for 100 percent of such revenues. Ultimately, this distorted revenues and the company had to restate its past financial statements.

Next, a short seller will pay attention to the "bill-and-hold policy." With this, a company will invoice a customer but retain the goods in the warehouse. This is a way to recognize revenues quicker. But it's an aggressive technique and tends to inflate profits. Besides, over time this can get expensive because of the storage costs for the inventory. Because of this, the SEC has strict requirements on how companies can account for a bill-and-hold policy. For the most part, the agency wants the company to have a legitimate reason, such as the need for temporary storage. An example of an abuser of the bill-and-hold method was the Sunbeam Corporation. Back in the late 1980s, the company not only stored large amounts of customer products but also provided discounts to encourage it. The SEC eventually discovered this and Sunbeam went bust.

Another area that allows for much discretion—as well as abuse—is the concept of principal versus agent relationships. If a company has ownership of its products and sells them, then it is a "principal." The company should be allowed to recognize the whole amount of the revenue in a transaction. Keep in mind that it has the risk of loss if something goes wrong. Sometimes, however, a company is merely a broker or a matchmaker. This would be the case with an operation like eBay because it does not even house the inventory. In this situation, it would be misleading for the broker to recognize the whole amount of the revenue. Instead, the company will recognize its fee or commission as revenue—which is often a much smaller amount (say less than 10 percent of the total revenues). Despite this, some companies try to show they are really principals so as to greatly boost revenues. This was common during the dot-com boom, when companies were trying to inflate their revenues.

Finally, acquisitions can be susceptible to "revenue manipulation." For instance, one trick is to have the target of an acquisition delay the reporting of its revenues. This means that the buyer will recognize more revenues earlier.

SPECIAL SITUATIONS

For certain types of industries, there are unique revenue situations. These can be helpful for short sellers in detecting emerging problems. Look at retailers and restaurants. In general, short sellers will not focus on overall revenues. Why? The reason is that they can be overstated by aggressive openings of new locations.

Rather, a short seller will want to focus on "same-store sales (SSS)" or "comparable store sales." With this metric, it is easier to measure the performance of a typical store. Basically, same-store sales has a core base of stores. In many cases, these are locations that have been in business for at least one year. So yes, it is possible for overall revenues to increase but same-store sales to fall. This would certainly get the attention of short sellers.

There is another metric that is helpful: "average revenue per store." A short seller will compare this with same-store sales. If SSS is increasing when revenue per store is falling, then this would be another sign of deterioration. Possible explanations include problems for new stores or the company has actually changed the definition of SSS, so as to inflate the numbers.

Another special situation for revenue recognition is software. A traditional software company will sell its offerings as a "license," which consists of an upfront fee and ongoing maintenance fees. However, as time goes by, a software company may have trouble getting new business. A sign of this would be a fall off in licensing fees. Interestingly enough, this can be masked because of the consistent underlying maintenance fees.

VENDOR FINANCING

"Vendor financing" is when a company provides credit for major customer purchases. This goes beyond accounts receivables. Rather, vendor financing is when a company essentially acts as a bank.

There are clearly legitimate reasons for vendor financing. For example, it is a way to help lock in customers and provide a value-added service. In fact, many top companies use this approach, such as Oracle and GE. Moreover, vendor financing can help boost margins. Why? The main reason is that a company can usually charge a premium price for the product. There will also be a profit from the ongoing interest and finance charges. But in some cases, companies get too aggressive with vendor financing. This is usually the case when a large portion of sales represent this method, say over 20 percent. In other words, there's a good probability that the company will not be able to pay back the vendor financing. The result is that the sales may be of low quality and the future may see write-downs. This is what happened to Lucent in 2001 to 2002, when the telecom industry went into a tailspin.

REVENUE VOLATILITY

What if there is a sudden spike in revenues? True, this usually gets bullish investors excited. However, short sellers will also be interested. Is the revenue real? Or is it an attempt to juice the stock price?

Generally, a short seller will be skeptical, especially when there are certain other factors at work. One factor would be if the company's industry is stagnating or is experiencing problems. Another red flag would be if there are no new product launches or major customer contracts. Ultimately, the company may be pumping up its revenues with accounting gimmicks.

EXPENSES

After the revenue amounts, the company will then list its expenses on the income statement. It's important to consider that all expenses were first assets. How? Let's take an example. Suppose you purchase a piece of equipment for $50,000. Under GAAP rules, you will list this on the balance sheet as an asset. But over time, you will get use from this equipment as it helps to generate revenues. As a result, you will need to steadily expense this asset over its useful life. This is called depreciation. Eventually, you will either depreciate the full value of the equipment or sell it. In some cases, it may become obsolete and the company will dispose of the property, taking a loss on the remaining value of the asset.

All in all, this is straightforward. But of course, companies will try to find ways to underestimate these depreciation expenses, which will keep asset values inflated, as well as allow for artificially higher profits.

COST OF GOODS SOLD

"Cost of goods sold (COGS)" shows those expenses that are directly related to selling a product. If a company provides services, this item is called "cost of sales (COS)," or "cost of revenues (COR)." In fact, the expenses for this category are fairly straightforward (that is, the cost of the professionals who provide the services). COGS, on the other hand, can be subject to interpretation. They generally include the compensation for the manufacturing workers and the costs of the inventory.

But after this, there are gray areas. Should the compensation for supervisors also be included? How about sales commissions? Basically, the inclusion or exclusion of such items depends on the discretion of management. Keep in mind, then, that in light of the importance of COGS—since it is part of the calculation of the widely followed gross-profit margin—the temptation is to minimize things. Yet, this can still be tough to do. Simply put, many of the expenses in COGS are essential for a company. Thus, if sales fall, it may be tough to move quickly enough to avoid losses.

GROSS PROFITS

The "gross profit" is the company's sales minus the cost of goods sold (COGS). From this, you can then calculate the "gross profit margin." This is as follows:

$$Gross\ Profit\ /\ Sales$$

Gross profit can vary widely from one industry to another. Take the software industry. It is fairly common for gross margins to be about 80 percent. The main reason is that the cost of distributing an intangible asset is fairly cheap. Margins are even better for companies that deliver their software via the Internet.

On the other hand, some companies have extremely low gross margins. These may be below 5 percent. Now, this is not necessarily bad. Keep in mind that Wal-Mart has gross profit margins of a few percentage points. But the company makes up for this with large volumes of sales. However, for short sellers, there will certainly be concern if a company has low margins when compared to its competitors. Basically, it was this that allowed Wal-Mart to put so many of its competitors out of business, such as Montgomery Ward.

SELLING, GENERAL, AND ADMINISTRATIVE COSTS

SG&A stands for selling, general, and administrative costs. These are often referred to as "overhead." When a company is having troubles, management will often look at cutting SG&A to boost profits. These can have an immediate impact as there are likely to be easy ways to cut costs.

But there are some problems when there are SG&A cuts. First, they tend to be one-time events. Do not expect the profit improvement to continue. Also, the cuts can ultimately harm the company as it loses its competitive edge. This would be the case with reductions in research and development, customer support, marketing, and so on.

THE HONEY POT

As we have seen, the world of accounting can be far from boring. Just look at some of the phrases to explain earnings manipulation, such as "honey-pot accounting." This was actually conjured up by the former executive of Network Associates. And yes, the company eventually became embroiled in an accounting scandal.

On its face, honey-pot accounting is not necessarily bad. It's actually when a company understates its earnings. For example, suppose XYZ Corp. is experiencing strong growth but management realizes it will slow down within a couple years. The company will find ways to create reserves against the earnings, which will lower them in the current period. Management may do this with a restructuring plan or acquisitions. Then, after a couple of years—when the growth indeed slows down—the company can release the reserves, which results in higher earnings.

This process is known as "smoothing earnings" and is not uncommon on Wall Street. Analysts like to see predictability in growth. But this is still a manipulation and the SEC has taken action against aggressive policies on reserves. As for short sellers, they will usually detect smoothing when a company consistently meets earnings' estimates for several years.

EARNINGS ESTIMATES AND WALL STREET ANALYSTS

Wall Street firms hire thousands of analysts. What's more, there are a variety of them.

Independent Analysts

One category includes the "independent analysts." These are individuals who get paid solely from the sales of their research, such as hedge funds and institutions. They typically work for boutique operations, which often have fewer than 50 employees. Independent analysts also tend to keep a low profile. After all, their clients do not want others to know their investment picks.

Buy-Side Analysts

Next, there are "buy-side analysts." They work for financial firms that invest money, like a mutual fund, hedge fund, or institution. Their focus is finding investments that generate the highest rates of returns.

Sell-Side Analysts

There are also "sell-side analysts." These are the ones you will typically see in the media like on CNBC. They work for investment banks, which provide advisory and capital-raising services to corporate clients. One of the ways to attract them is having analysts that cover the industries.

After the dot-com crash in 2000, the sell-side analyst community came under much pressure. It was not uncommon for analysts to have "buy" or even "strong buy" recommendations on stocks that quickly collapsed, such as Enron, Adelphia, and WorldCom. Interestingly enough, it was usually noted short sellers—such as Jim Chanos—who saw through these fraudulent companies. Why did analysts make these big misses? The irony is that many analysts understood the problems of the companies they covered but were under pressure to have positive ratings. Keep in mind that analysts work for financial firms that want to maintain client relationships with companies that are seeking funding or advisory work. If the analysts were too critical, these companies would likely go elsewhere. To counteract this problem, federal regulators instituted some changes to deal with the conflicts of interest. For example, there must be a "Chinese Wall" between investment banks and analysts. There are also restrictions on when an analyst can issue a report and disclosures about any equity interests.

Analysts' Advice and the Short Seller

Despite all this, analysts still have pressures to be upbeat. But ironically, this can be helpful for short sellers. If an analyst puts a "sell" recommendation on a stock, this is certainly a big deal. It is a gutsy call and the analyst probably has some good reasons. This is enough reason for a short seller to study the stock further, especially if the analyst is well-regarded and works for a top firm. An example is Meredith Whitney, who was working as a banking analyst at Oppenheimer. In October 2007, she predicted that Citigroup would cut or even eliminate its dividend so as to bolster its reserves. It was a controversial call and no other analysts followed. But she was proved correct as Citigroup announced the elimination of its dividend in the following quarter.

Because of major changes on Wall Street, the number of analysts has steadily declined. In fact, some companies have no analyst coverage. But for the remaining companies that have coverage, analysts are still important. Short sellers, in particular, can turn to one of several organizations that tabulate analyst forecasts and then put together consensus estimates. These firms include International Brokers' Estimate System (IBES), Thomson Reuters First Call, and Zack's Investment Research. When looking at this data, short sellers will focus on key areas. One is the "earnings estimates." These usually include the sales and earnings per share for the next quarter, as well as for the full year. In some cases, there may even be three- and five-year forecasts. An analyst will also have a price target on the stock.

Keep in mind that a company often puts out its own sales and earnings estimate, which are often conservative. And yes, the analysts' estimates are usually close. But a short seller will get concerned if several things occur. First, it is worrisome if a company has a major shortfall from its own and the analysts' forecasts. Is there a quick deterioration? Is it temporary? Another danger sign is when a company withdraws guidance. At a minimum, this is an indication that a company has little visibility in its underlying business.

ONE-TIME CHARGES

With the financial meltdown of 2008, many companies had major restructurings. These included actions like layoffs, sales of divisions, write-downs of inventory, and closure of business units. Then again, restructurings are common even during good times.

But of course, managements will try to minimize the perception that the restructuring is a bad thing. Instead, they will say that the changes are much-needed ones and will ultimately lead to a leaner organization. Managements will also say that the restructurings are one-time events. As a result, they are not part of the operating earnings. This makes the overall results look better than they really are. Despite the sugarcoating, however, the restructurings are still losses—and eat into a company's cash. It is also an admission that the industry is having problems or that management has not been able to execute its business plan effectively.

When looking at restructurings, short sellers will focus on some key areas. An important one is "recurring charges." It's interesting how some companies will often have one-time charges. In other words, short sellers will begin to wonder that a company is trying to find creative ways to hide major problems. Short sellers will be particularly interested if there is a restructuring at least once a year. Another trouble spot is an inventory write-down. Simply put, a company is unable to sell its products. This could be the result of a miscalculation of its demand. Or, more ominously, it could mean that the products are not competitive. The upshot could be long-term deterioration. Finally, a popular time to take a charge is during an acquisition. For example, suppose a company buys a struggling rival. The buyer may get the target to take a massive charge, so as to get the losses out of the way. In a way, this provides a clean slate for the buyer—and the loss does not show up on its income statement.

EARNINGS PER SHARE

"Earnings per share (EPS)" is a company's net income divided by the number of shares outstanding. For Wall Street investors and analysts, this is a critically important figure. In fact, if a company misses estimates by a penny or two, there can be a significant drop in the stock price. Why the sensitivity?

There are several reasons. First, a company should be able to make up for a small shortfall with the release of excess reserves. Or, a company may reduce the number of shares outstanding through buybacks. In other words, this may result in a misleading perception that the company is growing. But instead, management is really engaging in financial engineering. EPS is also the basis of the Price-Earnings (P/E) ratio, which is highly followed. It is calculated as:

Stock Price / Earnings per Share (EPS)

Even though it's fairly simplistic, this indicator is still quite useful. But there are some caveats. For example, suppose XYZ Corp. has a P/E ratio of 100. On its face, this would seem high. Think of it in these terms: a company will need to earn the same amount of earnings for 100 years to equate the current value of the stock. No doubt, this seems somewhat crazy. And it probably is. That is, the P/E ratio is overstating the valuation. This could be because of a recession or a temporary fall in the industry. But, when things return to normal, the EPS will go back to typical levels and the P/E ratio will look much better.

Another drawback of the P/E ratio is that it looks to the past. Yet investors are mostly forward-looking. Thus, if earnings are expected to surge in the next year, the valuation of the P/E ratio will likely be understated. To deal with these problems, investors have made refinements to the P/E ratio. Some investors will instead use a variation of the P/E ratio—that is, the P/E Growth (PEG) ratio. The ratio compares a company's Price-Earnings (P/E) ratio to the growth in its earnings per share (EPS).

A company's P/E ratio is likely to increase if the growth rate does as well. But of course, the reverse is true. However, there may be a delayed effect, especially for a company that has had a long history of strong growth. So to calculate the PEG ratio, you will first get a company's earnings growth rate. To do this, you can take the last three or four years of a company's EPS figures and compare them to the consensus EPS forecast for the next 12 months.

Next, you will compute the PEG ratio as follows:

P/E Ratio / Growth Rate

A short seller will look for situations where the P/E ratio is far ahead of the growth rate. For example: XYZ Corp. has a P/E ratio of 20 but a growth rate of 2 percent, giving it a PEG ratio of 10. All in all, this is a high number and the company will eventually need to grow much faster to justify its valuation.

Table 7-3 outlines some guidelines.

TABLE 7-3

How to React to P/E Ratios

0.50 or Lower	Buy
0.50 to 0.65	Look to buy
0.65 to 1.00	Hold
1.00 to 1.30	Look to sell
1.30 to 1.70	Consider shorting
1.70 or greater	Short

Another variation on the P/E ratio is the Forward P/E ratio. This is calculated as the stock price divided by the EPS for the next 12 months. It is usually based on the consensus earnings estimates from Wall Street analysts. True, this is far from perfect. But with a Forward P/E, you are factoring in future expectations. Thus, if the P/E is still high—relative to a company's peers and the overall market—then there could be a short-sale trade opportunity.

Investors will also use this variation:

Current P/E / Forward P/E

If the ratio is above 1, then there is lots of bullishness for the stock. If a short seller believes the sentiment is too optimistic—and the company will not be able to meet expectations—then there may be a short-sale prospect.

Just as seen in the previous chapter on balance sheets, the income statement is also subject to many assumptions and judgments. The result is that a company has a variety ways to manipulate the results. While there are various techniques to uncover these deceptions, there is another important disclosure: the statement of cash flows. This tends to be harder to manipulate. Because of this, a short seller will compare this to the income statement—which is yet another way to uncover attractive short-selling targets.

CHAPTER 8

Statement of Cash Flows

Key Concepts

- The basics of the cash flow statement
- Detecting problems
- Using ratios
- Screening stocks

Many investors think that profits and cash flows are the same thing. But this is far from the fact. Profit is an accounting concept and is subject to a variety of estimates and assumptions, as seen in Chapter 7. Cash flow, on the other hand, is really focused on showing how cash runs through a company. As a result, it can be harder for management to manipulate the numbers. But this does not imply that it is fraud-free. In fact, there are some tricks that managements use to inflate cash flows—though these attempts tend to be harder to pull off. Besides, investors usually focus on earnings rather than cash flows. So when it comes to financial statement manipulation, there is more emphasis on the income statement.

Despite all this, the cash flow statement is a must-read for short sellers. A cash shortage can be deadly for a company and result in a plunge in the stock price.

THE STATEMENT OF CASH FLOWS

Since the 1930s, public companies have had to disclose balance sheets and income statements. But it was not until 1988 that there was a requirement to provide the statement of cash flows—also known as a cash flow statement. Before then, a stock analyst had to find creative ways to calculate this. One was a simple formula:

$$Net\ Income + Depreciation = Cash\ Flow$$

Why add back depreciation? Keep in mind that depreciation is a non-cash expense. The fact is that the company has already paid cash for the asset—and is now taking periodic expenses to account for this. Interestingly enough, this simple cash-flow formula is still in use today and is somewhat useful, but it also can be misleading.

In order to sidestep the confusion brought about by the aforementioned formula, a short seller will instead focus on a company's statement of cash flows. This is really quite similar to an income statement, but it has different categories and does not use accrual accounting principles. The result is that it is much easier to see the inflows/outflows of cash. Because of this, there are occasional spikes and drops in the figures, especially on a quarter-by-quarter basis. This is why it is critical to look at overall trends, say six months to a year. In addition, a short seller will also account for seasonality. For example, some software companies get a large amount of cash flows in the fourth quarter because that's when customers often spend leftover budgets—and are also preparing for the upcoming year.

The statement of cash flows will have two formats: the direct and indirect method. The only difference between the two is the operating activities section. Table 8-1 shows the operating section for the direct method.

TABLE 8-1

Operating Section of the Statement of Cash Flows for Direct Method

Cash flows from operating activities	
Cash received from customers	$50,000
Cash paid to suppliers and employees	$20,000
Interest received	$1,000
Interest paid, net of amounts capitalized	$2,000
Income tax refund received	$1,500
Income taxes paid	$5,000
Other cash received (paid)	$1,000
Net cash provided by (used in) operating activities	$26,500

By contrast, Table 8-2 is a sample of the indirect method for operating activities.

TABLE 8-2

Operating Section of the Statement of Cash Flows for Indirect Method

Cash flows from operating activities	
Net income (loss)	$25,000
Adjustments to reconcile to net cash:	
Depreciation and amortization	$3,000
Estimate for doubtful accounts	$500
Changes in working capital	
Accounts receivable	$(8,000)
Inventory	$(2,000)
Prepaid expenses	$1,000
Accounts payable	$3,000
Cash flow from operations	$21,500

Shown in Tables 8-3 and 8-4, respectively, are the next two sections of the statement of cash flows. Again, notice that they are the same for both the direct and indirect methods.

TABLE 8-3

Investing Activities Section of the Statement of Cash Flows

Investing activities	
Capital Expenditures	($ 6,104)
Investments	($157)
Other cash flows from investing activities	($22,466)
Total cash flows from investing activities	($28,727)

TABLE 8-4

Financing Activities Section of the Statement of Cash Flows

Financing activities	
Dividends paid	$0
Sale/Purchase of Stock	($1,585)
Net borrowings	($1,638)
Other cash flows from financing activities	$0
Total cash flows from financing activities	($3,223)

While similar, the accounting authorities prefer the direct method. The main reason is the importance of understanding the operating activities, which is often the focus for analysis. The key piece of information is that you can *see* the actual cash from customers and any tax refunds. There are also disclosures of payments to vendors, suppliers, and employees. However, using the direct method is at the option of the company. And yes, the indirect method is fairly common.

The "Operating Activities" section shows the revenues from the core business, as well as the expenses used to generate them. If a company uses the indirect method, the calculation involves a variety of additions and subtractions based on the changes of key accounts. First, the depreciation and amortization will need to be added back. Again, this is because they are non-cash expenses. This is also the case with the allowance for doubtful accounts. It's an amount that is an estimated expense—but of course, no cash has left the company's coffers. Next, inventory will often have a big impact on cash flows. An increase in this item will represent an outflow of cash, and vice versa. Finally, accounts receivables will be a major part of a company's cash flows. An increase will represent a decline in cash, and vice versa. Simply put, a customer has yet to pay. Rather, this amount will hopefully be paid in the future, which will then increase cash flows.

While the "Investing Activities" and "Financing Activities" sections are not as important, short sellers will certainly analyze them. They provide detail on major investments, as well as the amounts raised from investors. For example, the "Investing Activities" section highlights the cash outlays for long-term assets (those that last longer than a year). Examples include equipment, software, and even the purchase of other companies. These are often referred to as "cap-ex" (for capital expenditures). On the other hand, when a company sells a capital asset, this is an inflow of cash. But this is not a common event, especially for smaller companies. Thus, when looking at the "Investing Activities" section, there will usually be cash outflows.

For many investors, there is a negative view on big increases in cap-ex. Of course, it reduces cash flows and can also be a risk. Will the new assets lead to growth? Investors, like Warren Buffett, prefer companies that have light cap-ex requirements. But another interpretation is that cap-ex shows that a company's growth prospects are bright. Just look at companies like Apple and Google. They generally increase cap-ex because their products are in high demand. So a short seller will be careful about trading a company that is ramping up cap-ex. Instead, there will be more interest when this line item is declining rapidly. It is usually a sign that a company is facing little growth opportunities and the core business may be deteriorating.

Finally, the "Financing Activities" section will show how a company raises capital from investors, such as with stock issuances, debt offerings, bank loans, and increased credit from vendors. These amounts will then be offset by outflows like dividends, share buybacks, and the repurchase of outstanding debt. Keep in mind that if a company is showing negative operating cash flows, then it probably has a positive amount from the "Financing Activities" section.

THE FOCUS ON OPERATING CASH FLOWS

As with long investors, short sellers will spend more time on the "Operating Activities" section. The main reason is that the "Operating Cash Flows" section provides an overall look at the success or failure of the business model. A classic example of this was during the dot-com bubble of the 1990s. Many companies had fancy Web sites and millions of users. But the operating cash flows were usually extremely negative and would never reach a positive number. The only way these companies stayed afloat was by raising money from investors, which was clearly apparent in the high amounts in the "Financing Activities" section. When it became nearly impossible to raise money, many dot-com companies went bust.

A key metric to look for is the operating cash flow margin. This is as follows:

$$Operating\ Cash\ Flows\ /\ Sales = Operating\ Cash\ Flow\ Margin$$

If the operating cash flow margin is growing, then the company would be a lousy short-sale prospect. On the other hand, if there is deterioration—or the margins are negative—then a short seller may have a good candidate. But a short seller will need to be careful. After all, management may attempt to overstate the operating cash flows. This usually means finding creative ways to shift expenses from operating cash flows to the other categories. Or, it could be transferring positive inflows from these other sections to the operating cash flow area.

As you can probably imagine, management has lots of discretion in terms of these classifications. Because of this, a short seller will dig into the different categories and see if there is anything that is suspect. One thing a short seller will look for is "factoring." This is when a company sells its accounts receivables for cash. Because of the risk of collecting the full amount, a company will get a discount for the sale of the asset. Furthermore, some companies will consider this to be operating cash flow. But for short sellers, this will be viewed as an aggressive approach. Instead, they will probably view this as a financing activity. Besides, factoring may be a sign of weakness. Why does the company need cash now? Are there problems with liquidity? Factoring may have another risk; that is, the company could ultimately be responsible for the debt if it is not paid. This often means future losses.

Another red flag with operating cash flows is acquisitions. When a company pays cash for another company, it is included in the "Investing" section of the cash flow statement. And yes, this is the appropriate method of accounting. But some companies engage in aggressive acquisitions, which certainly consume lots of cash. This is why a short seller will also calculate the cash flow after adjusting for acquisitions. If this is consistently negative, then the company is really having troubles with its cash flows.

Then, in some cases, a company will even change the definition of operating cash flows. The result is that the figure will be inflated. To detect the change, you will have to look at the footnotes of the financial statements. What's more, a company may inflate operating cash flows by delaying payments to vendors and suppliers. Why is this a problem? First of all, this cannot last for long. At some point, vendors and suppliers will rebel. They may start raising prices or holding back on supplies when markets get tough.

You can measure the payment cycle with the Day's Sales of Payables (DSP) ratio. Here is how it is calculated:

Accounts Payable / (Cost of Goods Sold × Number of Days in the Period)[1]

Finally, a short seller will look at volatility in operating cash flows. If the swings are large from quarter to quarter, then there may be manipulation. A classic example of this was Enron. Table 8-5 provides a look at its cash flows history, up until the company filed for bankruptcy.

---

[1] Recall that there are generally around 91.25 days in a quarter.

TABLE 8-5

Enron's Pre-Bankruptcy Cash Flows History

Time Period	Operating Cash Flows
Q1 2000	–$457M
Q2 2000	–$90M
Q3 2000	$674M
Q4 2000	$4,652M
Q1 2001	–$464M
Q2 2001	–$873M

QUALITY OF EARNINGS RATIO

All companies have a divergence between net income and cash flows. This is normal and inevitable because the two figures have different types of calculations. But a short seller will be alerted when the divergences are wide. To this end, he or she will look at the quality of earning (QE) ratio. This is as follows:

Operating Cash Flows / Net Income = QE Ratio

If the ratio is 0.50 or lower, then there is a disconnect between net income and cash flows. All in all, there's a good chance that a company is getting aggressive in how it accounts for its earnings.

Another helpful tool is to look at cash flow efficiency. As the name implies, this shows how well a company is managing its cash flows. Here's the formula:

(Current Assets − Cash and Cash Alternatives) / (Current Liabilities − Short-Term Debt) = Cash Flow Efficiency

For the most part, a short seller will want to see a low ratio, such as below 1.0. This means that a company is tying up its cash in assets like accounts receivables and inventory. (Note that the short-term debt includes notes payables, as well as the long-term debt that must be paid off within one year.)

DISCOUNTED CASH FLOW ANALYSIS

According to academics, discounted cash flow (DCF) analysis is considered the best method for valuing a company. The reason is that it not only accounts for the earnings, but it looks at the growth rates and makes adjustments for the present value of money.

To understand this, let's take a look at this in different steps. First, the equity markets are forward-looking. They are willing to invest their hard-earned money to get a future return, hopefully one that is higher than what they could get with a risk-free investment (such as a Treasury bill). This, by the way, is why a stock price may actually go up when the earnings fall. Basically, investors have anticipated that earnings would fall and have already "discounted" this into the stock price. In other words, then, investors are constantly estimating the future earning power of a company.

Some investors use "gut" instinct while others use sophisticated computer models. But when there are many investors looking at a stock, there is a valuation that is fairly realistic. Keep in mind, however, that investor valuation must account for the "time value of money." This refers to the simple concept that a person would rather have $1 today than $1 in 12 months. In other words, the future return will have a lower value. This means investors want to be compensated for this.

Discounted cash flow accounts for all these factors in a fairly complex formula, which usually requires the help of a spreadsheet. What's more, an analyst will typically use "free" cash flows, not "operating" cash flows. This is the operating cash flows minus the cap-ex. Another critical part of the DCF formula is the growth rate. Investors may be overly optimistic and believe the expected growth rate of the company is 25 percent, whereas you think it is 10 percent. If you are correct, you should have a solid short sale.

STOCK SCREENS

In the past three chapters, we have looked extensively at how short sellers analyze the income statement, the balance sheet, and the statement of cash flows. As you can see, there are many nuances and analytical approaches. Of course, the problem is how to use these tools so that it does not take too much time. There is certainly a risk of "paralysis by analysis."

One way to save time is to use a "stock screener." This is an online system that allows an investor to filter a database of public companies by using various metrics. For example, you could search for companies that have debt-to-equity ratios of over 50 percent and sales declines of more than 50 percent. Depending on the filters, the list may still be too long or even too short. In some cases, the criteria are so extreme that there are no companies that fit. So it takes time to refine a stock screener and produce a list that is manageable, say 15 to 20 companies. With this list, a short seller will then do deeper analysis. This will involve researching prior earnings releases, checking stock price charts, looking at recent developments, and so on. Through this process, the short seller will be pruning the list even more. Hopefully, he or she will have a high-quality group of short-sale candidates.

Keep in mind that there are hundreds of online screeners, including top ones from Yahoo! Finance, Smart Money, and MSN Money. Even though many are free, this does not mean they are not good enough for sound investment analysis. And speaking of Yahoo!, it actually has a top-notch offering. But it is a good idea to try out various screeners and find the one that works best for you. And if you still have problems, you can look at subscription-based screeners. These can be fairly affordable, such as costing $100 per year (this is the case with Morningstar). But at first, it's a good idea to use a trial offer and see if the screener has the capabilities you are looking for.

What are some important factors to consider? One is to make sure you have a screener that has a large database—say, one that includes the Nasdaq and NYSE stocks—and is refreshed frequently. Next, look for a screener that allows you to output the list to a spreadsheet. This makes it easier to conduct more analysis. Finally, some screeners may not allow you to create your own filters—instead, there are predefined ones.

So how do you set up your own screener to flag companies that are vulnerable for a drop? One filter to consider is from Professor Messod Beneish, who developed the M score. This is an extensive filter that tries to detect companies that are manipulating their financial statements. The M score has two versions, one that is based on eight variables and the other based on five. Because it is not as complicated—or tough for a screener— let's take a look at the latter. Here are the five variables:

1. **Day's Sales in Receivables Index (DSRI):** The annual change in the day's sales in receivables. The focus is to see if receivables and revenues are out of balance, which could mean there is earnings manipulation.

2. **Gross Margin Index (GMI):** The ratio of the gross margin over the past year. If this is greater than 1.0, then there has been deterioration.

3. **Asset Quality Index (AQI):** The ratio of the non-current assets—excluding property, plant, and equipment—to total assets over the past year. If this is over 1.0, then it may be an indication that the company is trying to defer its costs so as to inflate earnings. The reason is that the company is possibly capitalizing its costs.

4. **Sales Growth Index (SGI):** The ratio of sales over the past year. If this is above 1.0, then the company may be subject to accounting manipulation. The premise is that growth companies generally are those that engage in this type of activity.

5. **Depreciation Index (DEPI):** The ratio of depreciation over the past year. If this is below 1.0, then the company may be aggressively changing its depreciation policy and assumptions so as to improve profits.

With this data, you will then make the following calculation:

$$M = -6.065 + 0.823 \times DSRI + 0.906 \times GMI + 0.593 \times AQI + 0.717 \times SGI + 0.107 \times DEPI$$

If the M score is above –2.22, then there is a strong probability that a company is manipulating its financial statements. Based on Beneish's research, the success rate is a strong 76 percent.

While this formula is certainly useful, a good short seller will still use the other analytical techniques in this chapter. Before making a decision, a short seller needs to read through the statement of cash flows—and of course, the balance sheet and income statement—to gauge the overall position of the company. Kind of like a detective, you will try to spot clues where management is trying to conceal problems or hype things.

In the next chapter, we will move away from the fundamentals and instead look at technical analysis. This is a controversial area but is often a key tool for short sellers, especially when making short-term trades.

CHAPTER 9

Technical Analysis

Key Concepts

- Understanding charts and technical indicators
- Analyzing bear chart patterns, including the Head and Shoulders and the Double Top
- Using candlestick charts
- Looking at the Elliott Wave

When it comes to investment analysis, the primary focus is on the fundamentals—like revenues, earnings, and industry trends. But even this approach is suspect. According to the academic community, liquid markets are efficient and an investor cannot get above-market returns over the long haul. The main reason is that all new information about a stock is immediately embedded in the price. Academics also have little regard for another investment approach: "technical analysis." This technique involves analyzing chart and volume patterns to spot investment opportunities. The premise is that sentiment is reflected in these areas and that human nature is repetitive.

So what's the take from short sellers? For the most part, they will tend to focus on fundamental analysis and believe that markets are inefficient enough to find excellent investment opportunities. But some short sellers will also use technical analysis. They will often focus on a combination of fundamental analysis and technical analysis. For example, a short seller analyzes XYZ Corp. and thinks it is deteriorating. But the stock keeps steadily moving upwards. In this case, a short seller may wait for a chart pattern that indicates that bears are coming into the stock.

In other words, technical analysis is essentially a way to get an entry point for a short-sale trade. Or, a short seller may use charts to determine the price level to exit a trade. This would be the case if the chart shows a bottoming pattern.

THE BASICS

While some technicians will look at long-term chart patterns, the focus is still usually on the "short term." This means making a trade and staying with the position for a period from a couple of days to a month or so. The reason is that trends can change quickly. In fact, there are hundreds of patterns for technical analysis, making things complicated. The good news is that these can be boiled down into two main categories.

First, the investor looks at common chart patterns, like the "Double Top" and the "Head-and-Shoulders" formation. Secondly, an investor will also compare these to volume levels, which can help to confirm a buy or sell signal. Technical analysis also involves various indicators which are mathematical ratios and algorithms. For example, an "oscillator" will have a value that ranges from 0 to 100.

VOLUME INDICATORS

"Volume" is the number of shares bought and sold in a stock. The saying is that "volume precedes the price." So if there is a growing number of sale orders, the stock price will likely trend downward.

To detect these movements, there are helpful volume indicators. Consider "On Balance Volume (OBV)." Legendary investor Joe Granville developed this during the early 1960s and it is expounded upon in his book *New Key to Stock Market Profits*.

To get the OBV, you will first add the volume on the days the stock price is higher than the day before. Next, you will subtract the volume on the days the stock price is lower than the day before. The cumulative total is then provided on a chart and is called the "OBV line." To use this indicator, a short seller will look at a chart pattern and then compare it to the OBV line. If the OBV line is dropping, then this is an indication that bearishness is coming into the stock. As a result, an upward trend may not continue for awhile.

There is also another helpful volume indicator: the "Accumulation/Distribution Line (ADL)," which essentially corrects some of the flaws in the OBV line. After all, it is not necessarily true that the closing price should be the indicator of bullishness or bearishness. So the creator of the ADL indicator, Marc Chaikin, focused on the "midpoint price." This is the daily high plus the daily low divided by two. If the close is higher than the midpoint, then there is bullish sentiment and the stock is undergoing "accumulation." As for the alternative, this would mean the stock is seeing a "distribution," which is negative and may be a good short-sale candidate.

CHART BASICS

For technical analysis, a chart can be for any time frame. These include intraday trading to yearly trends. Also, a chart will be made up of vertical bars, which usually mark the trading for one day. Figure 9-1 is an example for the stock of Oracle.

On this chart, each vertical bar has two horizontal bars, which are called "tick marks." The tick mark that extends to the left is the "opening price." Interestingly enough, this is usually not the actual first trade of the day. It is probably an average of the first few trades. This is why there may be discrepancies between quote data services. The tick mark that extends to the right is the "closing price." This is often considered the most important part of the chart. The reason is that the closing price is the culmination of a full day's worth of trading, in which investors have had a chance to digest news. Moreover, it is easier to see the impact of the volume. If the stock falls at the close—with heavy volume—it may be an indication of further weakness. Some technicians will develop charts that focus only on the daily closes.

As for the vertical bar, the top represents the highest trade for the day. If the high of the day is at the same price as the open—or close to it—and the stock winds up lower at the close, this is an

FIGURE 9-1

Sample Stock Chart, Oracle

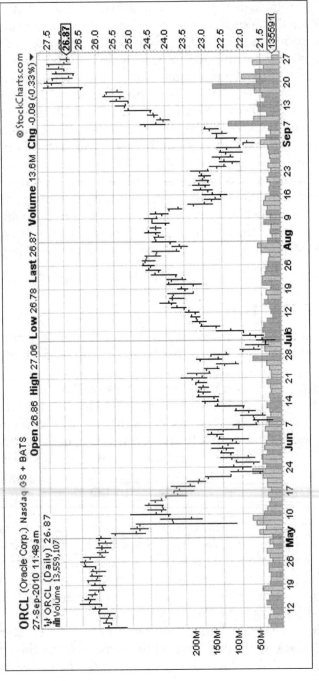

Chart courtesy of StockCharts.com.

indication of bearishness in a stock. And yes, the bottom of the vertical bar is the lowest trade for the day. For a short seller, he or she will look for patterns where the lows are getting lower over time. Underneath this price chart, there will usually be a graph of the volume for the stock. And some technical analysts will add other indicators, like the ADL indicator.

It should be no surprise that charts can be misleading, especially for volatile stocks. Consider Google. After the company came public in the summer of 2004, the stock price surged over the next couple of years. But for technical analysis, the chart exaggerated the move. The reason is that the axis is not scaled properly. For example, the size between the stock price at $100 to $200 is different from $200 to $300 and so on. To deal with this problem, you can instead use a "log-scale chart." This adjusts things so the vertical changes are the same for each percentage change move.

INTERPRETING CHARTS

Of course, there are many ways to interpret charts—as well as controversy as to what approaches work. But there are some key principles for technical analysis. First of all, there is "the support level," which is the price where buyers will start to take a position in the stock. Figure 9-2 provides a look at Google's chart, which shows that the support level is roughly at $435.

The Resistance Level

At this point, a short seller may want to cover the position, especially if there is already a profit. Or, if he or she thinks there will be more deterioration, the price fall could be substantial. This is often the case when a stock price breaks through its support level. It's usually considered highly bearish. Above the support level is "the resistance level," which is the price at which investors sell the stock. For Google's chart, this is $510. When a stock moves above the resistance level, there could be a spike in the price. This certainly happened with Google's stock as it broke the $510 resistance level. After this, there was a rally in the stock.

FIGURE 9-2

Sample Stock Chart, Google

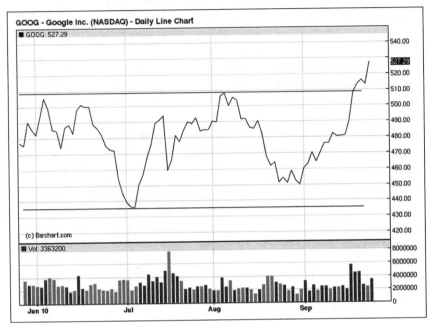

Chart courtesy of Barchart.com.

The Uptrend

A short seller will also want to gauge the overall trends. The most dangerous, of course, is "the uptrend." This is when a stock makes several higher lows and higher highs. All in all, the stock is showing strong momentum, which is fairly easy to detect on the chart since the lines are going mostly upward. But if the stock price begins to break below this uptrend line there could be trouble. That is, investors believe the valuation is too high. For some short sellers—who are willing to tolerate high risk—this may be a good point to short a stock (say if the stock is a couple of percentage points below the uptrend line).

The Neutral Trend

Then there is "the neutral trend," in which the number of highs and lows are roughly the same. In this situation, investors are waiting for a move to break out of this trend, either on the downside or upside.

The Downtrend

Finally, a short seller will look for "the downtrend," which involves a series of lower highs and lower lows. This clearly shows that investors are highly negative on the stock. For short sellers, this may be a sign to take a short position or to hold onto an existing short position.

RETRACEMENTS

It's common for investors to get overly bullish or bearish on a stock. When this happens, the price will eventually back off because of profit-taking. This is known as a "retracement" or a "correction."

When it comes to the overall market, a typical retracement is a 10-percent fall from the high (also known as a correction). For a short seller, this certainly will be a big opportunity to make some nice profits. And it can be quick, with the retracement happening over a couple of months or so. Sometimes a retracement will be more serious and could lead to a major reversal. If the drop is 20 percent or more, it would mean there is a bear market. No doubt, this is the most ideal situation for a short seller.

When it comes to an individual stock, the retracement may be more severe. Consider the "Gann retracement." Based on the findings of an investor from the early 1990s, a retracement for a stock would be roughly 50 percent from the original move from the low to the high. For example, say XYZ Corp. has gone from $30 to $60 and then runs into resistance. A Gann retracement would see the stock go back to $45, which would be a 25-percent return for a short seller.

Other investors rely on so-called "Fibonacci numbers" when measuring a retracement. Based on the mathematical theories, this is a sequence of numbers that start with 1, 1, 2, 3, 5, 8, 13, and so on. What's the significance? Keep in mind that Fibonacci sequences are often seen in nature—like hurricanes—and can help with predictions. So a trader, Ralph Elliott (1871–1948), studied Fibonacci numbers and applied them to investment strategies. He realized that he could put together waves, which he called "Elliott Waves." From this, he came up with two retracement waves, which were either 38-percent or 62-percent drops.

Regardless of these various approaches, retracements are still major drops in a stock price and are enough to get the interest of short sellers. But in terms of taking advantage of a retracement, a short seller will need to find reversals in charts and other technical indicators. Some of the common ones include moving averages, the Head and Shoulders, and the Double Top.

MOVING AVERAGES

There are two types of moving averages. The most common is the "simple moving average (SMA)." You add the closing prices for a stock for, say 20 days, and then divide this by 20. Every day, you will then recalculate the SMA.

Then there is the "exponential moving average (EMA)." This is a weighted average and involves two steps. First, you will start by using a stock's SMA. Then you will come up with a weighting factor, such as focusing more on the first third of the moving average. In other words, the EMA should react faster to recent activity compared to the SMA.

Which moving average should you use? A short seller likes to focus on the EMA and use a time period of 150 to 200 days. If the EMA falls below the current stock price, this is a bearish indicator. This is known as the "Death Cross."

Another useful moving-average indicator is the "Moving Average Convergence-Divergence (MACD)." In the late 1970s, investor Gerald Appel created this tool to measure "momentum" in a stock. And for the most part, the calculation is fairly simple. The MACD tracks two moving averages and subtracts the longer one (26-day) from the shorter one (12-day). With this indicator, there will be a zero line. From this, the MACD will converge—get closer to the line—or diverge. If the MACD is positive, then there is upside momentum in the stock, and vice versa.

There are two main bearish signals. One is the bearish "centerline crossover." With this, the centerline essentially moves below zero. However, it is important for the centerline to have been above zero for a couple of weeks. This means that there is a sudden move of downward momentum. There is also "negative divergence," which is when the MACD centerline falls yet the stock price increases or remains stable.

THE DOUBLE TOP AND
THE HEAD AND SHOULDERS

The "Double Top" is perhaps the most common bear-type chart. There are three phases.

- **The first phase is the First Top:** At this point, investors are optimistic about the stock and aggressively buy up the shares. But the stock eventually hits a high and then falls back to the support level.

- **The next phase is the Second Top:** Again, investors see lots of potential in the stock and drive it upwards. But the price hits a resistance level—which is usually below the prior peak. In other words, it is getting tougher to sustain the rally. Besides, some short sellers may be coming into the stock.

- **The last phase is the Reversal:** This is when the stock hits the support level and breaks through it. This is a highly negative signal and is a favorite for short sellers.

Basically, the chart will have an M shape, as seen in Figure 9-3.

A variation of the Double Top is the "Head and Shoulders." The difference between the two is that there are three peaks in the "Head-and-Shoulders" chart, with the middle one being higher than the ones on the left and right sides. Also, when the stock price hits the support level on the right side, there will be a reversal as the stock price falls.

OSCILLATORS

"Oscillators" are quite helpful for technical analysis because they show signs when a stock is overbought or oversold. These can be confirmation points for chart patterns or other indicators. One of the first oscillators came from investor George C. Lane, who devel-

FIGURE 9-3

M-Shaped Double Top

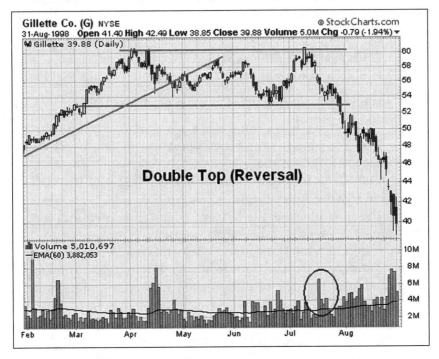

Chart courtesy of StockCharts.com.

oped the "stochastic oscillator" back in the 1950s. His main purpose was to try to find a way to show momentum in a stock. With
this, an investor could spot *reversals*, either on the bull or bear side.
The "stochastic" is a somewhat complex formula. But for the most
part, it involves analyzing the lowest lows and the highest highs of
a stock. This is over a 14-point period of time. And a period can be
in days, weeks, or months.

The stochastic will have two lines on a chart. One is called
"%K" and the other is called "%D." When the stochastic reaches 80
or above, this is a sign that a stock is overbought. Although, for short
sellers, this is not necessarily a time to short. If a stock has lots of
momentum, it may keep up the pace for some time. Rather, a short
seller may wait for the stock to come back to 80 or so. At this point,
the momentum is slowing and the stock may be poised for a fall.

Another useful oscillator is the "Bollinger Band," which is the creation of famed investor John Bollinger. His oscillator involves two lines that move above and below a 21-day moving average. The idea is to measure the overall volatility in the stock. That is, if the bands contract, volatility is lessening, and vice versa. Actually, for a short seller, he or she will want to first see a stock undergo a "contraction" of its Bollinger Bands. Then there will be a wait-and-see period to get a sense of the direction of the stock. If the move is on the downside, this can be a trigger for a short-sale position.

Next, short sellers will also use another helpful oscillator, called the "Relative Strength Indicator (RSI)." This detects the extremes in *sentiment* for a stock. If the RSI is at 30 or below, then the stock is oversold. Or, if the RSI is over 80, then it is overbought. However, a short seller will usually wait for the RSI to go into a downtrend and then consider a trade when the indicator goes below 70. Another short signal is when a stock hits a new high yet the RSI does not confirm it.

TOP-DOWN ANALYSIS

Technical analysis is not just for evaluating an individual stock. For example, you can use these chart techniques for commodities, currencies, exchange-traded funds (ETFs), and options. Or you can use technical analysis for a "top-down analysis." This means looking at the performance of a sector, such as autos or steel. If there is weakness, you can then short the industry with an ETF or you can select one or several companies within the sector. Some of the helpful techniques for the top-down approach include the crossover of the 200-day moving average, the Double Top or Head-and-Shoulders patterns, and breaks below the Relative Strength Indicator (RSI) line.

CANDLESTICK CHARTS

Technical analysis is a recent phenomenon. In fact, this approach did not get much visibility until the 1970s and 1980s, when computer technologies became widespread and it was easier to develop investment models. But there is one technical analysis method that has deep roots: candlestick charts. The origins go back as far as sixteenth-century Japan. Back then, traders would use candlestick charts to help predict the movements in rice prices. Unlike other chart patterns, candlestick charts are fairly easy to interpret. The various patterns have descriptive names—which makes the system memorable.

A key to candlestick charts is getting a feel for the overall sentiment. Often, this is based on the size of the bars. For a candlestick chart, each bar usually represents one trading day. The bar will have a box in the middle and a line extending at the top and the bottom. The size of the box is based on the open and close—called the "real body." If the close is higher than the open, the real body will be white or else it will be black. So if you see many black real bodies that are getting longer, this is certainly a bearish signal. The top line—called the "upper shadow"—indicates the high. The bottom line—called the "lower shadow"—indicates the low.

Like technical analysis, candlestick charts have similar patterns. One is the "resistance level." If the trend has been upwards but has stalled—with larger bars—then it is an indication that the stock price has hit an upper level. There is also a "support level." This is when the prices have been in a downward trend but the recent action has seen larger bars. In this case, buyers are coming into the stock for support.

Figure 9-4 is an example of a candlestick chart.

However, going beyond this, there are some important candlestick formations that short sellers will focus on. These include the following:

- **Doji:** Here the real body is small—and getting smaller. In isolation, this does not mean much. A doji shows that the market is neutral. But if the stock has been in an uptrend and has moved into a doji state, it is a sign that momentum is slowing and a fall may ensue.
- **Engulfing Bearish Pattern:** When a stock is in an uptrend, there will be a sudden shift. The real body will turn black and be much larger than the prior white body.
- **Umbrella:** You will see two main characteristics. First, there will be a spinning top at the high end of the trading range. This is when the real body is small. Next, the candlestick will have a lower shadow that is a minimum of twice the size of the real body. If you find an umbrella

FIGURE 9-4

Sample Candlestick Chart

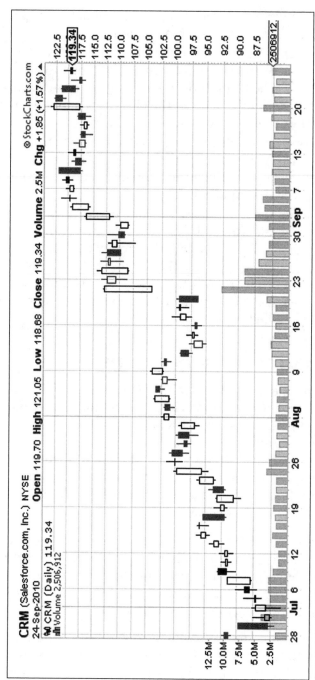

Chart courtesy of StockCharts.com.

pattern when the stock is in the uptrend, then expect a fall in the price. This is called a "hanging man."

- **Dark Cloud Cover:** With the stock in an uptrend, the candlestick will go from a large white body to a black body. For the black body, the open must be at the high of the white candlestick and the close at roughly the white candlestick's middle area.
- **Harami Line:** This shows a decline in momentum, which could mean a bearish phase for the stock. The harami has a small real body, which is essentially within the confines of the preceding candlestick.
- **Evening Star:** Several candlestick patterns involve a star. This is located much higher than the preceding candlestick. It's really an indication of a reversal of a pattern. A bearish one is the "evening star," since the location is much lower than the previous candlestick. Another is a "shooting star," which has a small real body and is at the lower price range.

THE ELLIOTT WAVE PRINCIPLE

In various articles and a book called *Nature's Laws*, Ralph Elliott set forth a comprehensive approach to predicting market moves. He believed that there was a consistent pattern of investor sentiment, going from negative to positive.

The Elliott Wave is for a variety of trends, whether multi-centuries or multi-decades, to several weeks or even hours. All in all, it can get quite complicated and there are often differing interpretations. But there are two main Elliott waves.

- **The Impulse Wave:** This can either be a bull or bear phase. Within this wave are five sub-waves. Two of the waves will move against the main thrust of the trend.
- **The Corrective Wave:** This wave represents a retracement. Within this wave are three sub-waves.

Perhaps the most well-known proponent of the Elliot Wave principle is Robert Prechter. He developed his theories as a market technician at Merrill Lynch and then published a groundbreaking book, *The Elliot Wave Principle* (1978). He actually predicted the huge bull market in the 1980s, as well as the stock market crash of 1987. However, since then, the predictions have not been as strong. Despite all this, the Elliott Wave has many top supporters, including the hedge-fund legend, Paul Tudor Jones. In fact, he is an avid follower of chart reading and indicators. The result is that he has made billions of dollars for his investors and himself.

THE HINDENBURG OMEN

"The Hindenburg Omen" attempts to predict a stock market crash and is perhaps the most feared chart pattern in technical analysis. Yes, the name comes from the tragic destruction of the famous German zeppelin on May 6, 1937. The creator of the Hindenburg Omen is Jim Miekka, who is a blind mathematician. His system relies on a variety of technical indicators that must be confirmed on the same day and the focus is on the New York Stock Exchange.

Hindenburg Omen Parameters

The ten-week moving average is rising.

The McClennan Oscillator is negative.

The daily number of new 52-week highs and new 52-week lows must both be greater than 2.2 percent of the total issues traded.

The 52-week highs cannot be more than twice the new 52-week lows.

If all these indicators are triggered, then there is a confirmed Hindenburg Omen. But within the next 36 days, there needs to be yet another confirmation. If so, the markets could be poised for a crash. In fact, the indicator has foreshadowed every market crash since the mid-1980s. Then again, there have been a variety of false signals.

FLASH CRASH AND DARK POOLS

On May 6, 2010, the Dow Jones Industrial Average (DJIA) plunged nearly 1,000 points within 20 minutes, representing close to $1 trillion in lost value. This started at 2:42 p.m. Up until this point, the market was down moderately. Investors were still concerned about the problems with the Greek debt crisis. Despite this, there was no catalyst to explain the plunge, known as the "Flash Crash." It appeared to be a random event. But could this be possible if the markets are indeed efficient? Keep in mind that, by the end of the day, the Dow recouped more than 600 points. Something else to consider is that some top companies saw unbelievable declines in their stock prices. For example, the shares of Accenture and Exelon fell to one cent. Then there was Apple, which saw its stock price surge to over $100,000.

So what happened? The whole answer may remain a mystery (this is even the case with the stock market crash of 1987). But there are some major contributors. One is the influence of high-frequency traders. These investors use computer algorithms to make trades, which can involve buy, sell, and short positions within milliseconds. While hedge funds are a big part of high-frequency trading (HFT), it is also common for institutional funds like insurance companies and even mutual funds. Consider that nearly three-quarters of trading comes from HFT. Another big factor is the "dark pools," which involves trading between electronic networks. The advantage is that the traders—and transaction amounts—are not disclosed, which is certainly attractive for traders who do not want others to see their actions.

Unfortunately, the Flash Crash had a negative psychological impact on investors. Can markets be trusted? It was certainly a legitimate concern. But the impact was also significant for technical analysis. First of all, the wide swings in trading gave off false signals in charts, disrupting moving average patterns, relative strength indexes (RSIs), and so on. Investors were wondering if they needed to adjust their charts for the volatility. Next, there were concerns about volume. If dark pools were a major force on Wall Street, are technical indicators picking up true volume? To deal with these problems, the SEC has implemented a variety of reforms.

Despite all this, technical analysis is still thriving on Wall Street. Even though we could only provide a basic introduction in this chapter, you still have some strong tools to make short-sale decisions. Over time, you will then delve into other techniques or focus on those you feel most comfortable with. In the next chapter, we will go beyond focusing on stock selection techniques and look at ways to predict bear markets.

CHAPTER 10

Detecting Bear Markets

Key Concepts

- Understanding bear markets
- Indicators to predict bear markets
- Looking at the impact of recessions, depressions, and deflation

While market timing is often criticized, many top investors use this strategy. In fact, it is important for short sellers. The main reason is that the biggest profits often come during bear markets, when most stocks fall. There are many market timing systems available, with varying results. And yes, many investors—and academics—believe that they generally do not work.

Markets are supposed to be efficient, at least over the long run. This theory is known as the "efficient market hypothesis (EMH)" and has roots that go back to the 1950s. The pioneers of the EMH are Eugene Fama and Kenneth French, both from the University of Chicago. The main premise is that "the stock market is random." You have just as good a chance at picking a stock as you do flipping a coin. Why is this so? The key reason is that the EMH assumes that all available information is instantly imbedded into the stock price. The result is that it is impossible to consistently beat the market.

Needless to say, this is disheartening to portfolio managers, who earn huge compensation packages for picking the right investments. Despite this, there is much factual support for EMH. Consider that it is mostly the case that portfolio managers—at least for mutual funds—lag the market. Because of this, there has been a strong trend toward "index funds." Such investments track the benchmarks and have rock-bottom fees. Yet the fact remains that there are investors who have indeed consistently beaten the markets. Some include George Soros, Paul Tudor Jones, and Stanley Druckenmiller. They have done this by being flexible in their strategies, which often involves short selling.

BEAR MARKETS

The origins of the phrase "bear market" are somewhat sketchy. But it appears that it goes back to the 1600s, when stock exchanges started to emerge. It seems that bear market derived from London bearskin jobbers. They would sell bearskins before the bears were caught. In fact, "bear" also became a word for short selling, since a jobber sold something he or she did not yet have!

Whatever the origins, a "bear market" is when prices are generally falling. No doubt, this can be grueling for long investors. For example, the stock market will often have a gradual fall, which eats into returns. The result is that many investors will not shift their money out of the market—or short it—until it is too late. Indeed, a bear market will often end in a "capitulation." This is when most investors have given up and believe that there is no hope. Pessimism has reached intense levels.

So what is the official definition of a bear market? Yet again, it is somewhat fuzzy. But perhaps one of the most popular definitions is a market that falls 20 percent or more during at least a two-month period. Although, the fall can easily be much more, say 40 percent to 50 percent or more.

But there are also different types of bear markets. The most painful is the "secular bear market," which is a long-term bear market. It could last ten years or more. Actually, some investors believe that the U.S. markets have been in the midst of a secular bear market since 2000. Examples include:

Bear Markets of the Twentieth Century

1901–1920	20 years
1929–1932	4 years
1937–1941	5 years
1966–1981	16 years

Next, a market may have a "short-term bear market"—which is known as a "crash." This is a fall of 10 percent or more, which can happen in just a few days. However, a crash is fairly rare. Finally, a market may have a "correction." This is a 10-percent fall that occurs over a period of a couple of months. A correction may happen in either a bull or bear market.

COMMON THEMES OF A BEAR MARKET

When looking at the history of bear markets over the past 100 years, there are some common factors. All of these factors have not necessarily been present for each phase, but at least one of the following factors helped trigger a bear market:

- **The first factor is "deflation":** This is a general fall in the prices in the economy. It's a horrible condition as it tends to feed on itself. Consumers will hold off buying goods and services since the expectation is that prices will fall. On the other hand, businesses will cut back on production because of the lack of demand. The result is usually a "depression," which happened during the 1930s in the United States and during the 1990s in Japan. As sales and earnings collapse, the stock market will go into the bear phase.

- **Another factor is when a market reaches historically high price-earnings ratios:** This is an indication that valuations are at unsustainable levels. This was certainly the case before the bear markets in 1966, 1973 to 1947, and 2000 to 2002. What level is too high? Consider that high levels of P/E ratios can last for some time, which happened from 1994 to 1998. However, when the Standard & Poor's (S & P) 500 sports a P/E of 20 or over, the markets have hit the danger zone. It will get tougher for companies to keep growing their earnings to justify the valuations.

- **The final factor is the inverted yield curve:** Basically, a "yield curve" is a graph of the yields of short-term to long-term bonds (up to 30 years). In a normal economic environment, the graph will have an upward slope. After all, a bank will borrow money from depositors at a low rate and lend the money at higher rates, creating a profit. But when there is an inverted yield curve, it is nearly impossible for banks to make money. The upshot is that they will pull back on lending and boost their reserves. It is the Federal Reserve that creates the inverted yield curve. The goal is to reduce economic activity, such as when inflation is getting problematic. However, this is not an easy process and a recession can easily be the outcome.

Again, a bear market will have one or two of the above factors. But there was one time when all three occurred: the bear market from 1929 to 1930. During this time, the Dow Jones Industrial Average plunged 89 percent.

MARKET-TIMING SYSTEMS

When it comes to market-timing systems, there are many approaches. Yet it can be frustrating to find one that works—and which is manageable to track. This is why it is important to focus on the top investors, who have long-term track records. One of the best is Martin Zweig. With a Ph.D. in finance, Zweig got his start as a financial newsletter writer. Because of his strong track record, he even became a TV personality and launched several closed-end and open-end funds. And even though he developed his methods during the 1970s and 1980s, they are still relevant today.

To get a sense of how his indicators work in the real world, let's take an example: On September 25, 1987, Zweig advised his clients that the market would plunge and recommended an interesting strategy: buy a put option on the stock market that was 8 percent out-of-the-money and would expire in mid-November. He advised that this represented 1 percent of the portfolio. On its face, it was a risky bet because the market would have to fall by more than 8 percent within the next two months, which was certainly a major move. But then again, if the trade failed, the loss would still only be 1 percent of the portfolio. Zweig considered this a "crash" insurance policy.

Of course, the bet paid off and the trade resulted in a staggering 2,075-percent return. For the portfolio, the profit was 20.8 percent, which offset the 7-percent losses on the remaining part of his positions. In all, his strategy resulted in a 9-percent gain on Black Monday. Zweig's original goal was to hedge the portfolio against an event that—based on his indicators—had a high probability of occurring. But in light of the extreme volatility in the markets, he was able to generate a substantial profit. In fact, this is common in times of instability—in which a hedge can turn into a leveraged trade.

So what is Zweig's marketing-timing system? It is fairly straightforward and easy to follow. He also is broad in his approach. He looks at monetary policy, technical analysis, and investor sentiment.

MONETARY POLICY

While a country's economic policy is complex, it still only involves two main parts. First, there is "fiscal policy." This includes the spending and tax initiatives. Such actions can have a significant impact on industries, such as health care and the military contractors. But for investors, fiscal policy is not necessarily helpful for market timing. One reason is that it is difficult to determine the impact of the various policies. Just look at the huge fiscal stimulus after the financial meltdown of 2008. While it helped to get the U.S. economy out of the recession—and perhaps even avoid a depression—the unemployment rate continued to remain high.

Instead, "monetary policy" is likely to be more helpful for investors. This involves the actions of the Federal Reserve (the Fed), which has the power to change interest rates and money supply in the U.S. economy. The Fed also has the authority to be the "lender of last resort." In a financial crisis, the Fed will come into the markets and provide cash to this system. The impact of monetary policy can be quick and substantial. Again, in 2008, the Fed injected over $1 trillion into the U.S. economy. By the following year, the stock market surged.

Of course, for short sellers, they will look at when the Fed tightens credit in the economy. When this happens, the markets can go into a bear phase from one to three years—or more.

Higher interest rates do this because of a variety of factors. First, there is competition for investor dollars. As yields rise, fixed-income securities become more attractive. So investors will start to unload stocks and move their funds into these securities. And in light of the global financial markets, the impact can be massive and quick. Next, higher interest rates will increase the costs for companies. In other words, if a company wants to expand, the interest costs will be higher. The impact will be particularly tough on capital-intensive industries like the airlines, utilities, and so on. Finally, consumers will also get squeezed. Simply put, higher interest rates will make it tougher for them to continue their spending, especially for high-ticket items.

As for Zweig, he looks at a variety of Fed indicators. But there are two main factors. One is the "discount rate." This is the interest rate the Fed charges member banks to borrow from the "discount window." Banks will access this source of funds when they need to boost reserves, which becomes more important when interest rates increase and the economy slows down. According to Zweig, just one increase in the rate—either 0.50 percent to 1 percent—is enough to be considered bearish. This will last for six months until there is another increase. Then there is the "reserve requirement," which is the amount of cash a bank must set aside. It is rare for the Fed to increase this rate. Thus, when it happens, it is a highly bearish signal for the stock market.

Keep in mind that—since Zweig developed these indicators—there have been major changes in the markets. But his Fed indicators are still valid. It is also worth looking at other approaches from top market prognosticators.

The Fed Model

Investment strategist Dr. Edward Yardeni created the Fed Model. His premise was that there is a tug-of-war between yields on bonds and total returns on stocks. When there is an imbalance, the stock market may be poised for a change—either bullish or bearish.

The Fed Model compares the yield on the 10-year Treasury to the S&P 500 forward earnings yield. The "forward earnings yield" is the one-year earnings per share forecast for the S&P 500 divided by the value of the S&P 500. If there is a difference, Yardeni recommends buying the higher-yielding investment and selling—or shorting—the lower one.

There are variations on the Fed Model. For example, investor David Merkel uses the Corporate BBB bond rate instead of the ten-year Treasury bond. With this, he requires that stocks need to yield at least 2.5 percent to 3.0 percent higher than the corporate rate to compensate for the risk.

The Treasury-Eurodollar Spread

Another helpful Fed indicator is the "Treasury-Eurodollar (TED) Spread." This is the relationship between the London Interbank Offered Rate (LIBOR) and the 90-day Treasury yield. The LIBOR is what global banks charge each other and is quoted in eurodollars. It is the base rate of a broad array of financial instruments like mortgages, business loans, and so on. The TED spread is usually minimal and does not change much. But if there is a sudden spike, then global bankers are getting jittery and more risk-averse. The result could be a tightening of the credit markets and a slowing of the global economy.

TECHNICAL ANALYSIS

Momentum can drive markets and the trend can easily last for a few years. And yes, Zweig has a saying for this: "The trend is your friend." This is really about technical analysis, which focuses only on price and volume, but Zweig deems price to be the most important factor. For the most part, strength begets strength, whether on the upside or downside. When it comes to momentum, the indicators are usually for detecting major bull phases.

The Value Line Index

Zweig does have one simple method for gauging downward forces. This is when the "Value Line Index"—which tracks 1,700 stocks on the New York Stock Exchange and Nasdaq—falls 4 percent or more during one week. All in all, it is a highly negative sign and the markets could be poised for a bear phase. There are also some other helpful indicators.

Trading Index

One helpful indicator is the "TRIN (Trading Index)." Back in the late 1960s, Richard Arms developed this indicator. It looks at the comparison between those stocks advancing to those declining, while including the volume. Here's the formula:

(Number of Advancing Stocks/Number of Declining Stocks) /
(Advancing Volume/Declining Volume)

In general, there will not be much activity in the TRIN. But of course, this is not the case when volatility increases. For short sellers, they will look for a TRIN of 1.20 or higher. It is a sign that the market is overbought.

The Volatility Index

There is also the "Volatility Index (VIX)." Launched in the early 1990s, the VIX has turned into a widely-watched indicator. It measures the daily change in implied volatility in the S&P 500. If there is a sudden spike in the VIX, it could mean a change in direction of the market. Although the VIX is not really good in identifying long-term bear or bull markets, it is good at gauging the trend for the next couple of months.

INVESTOR SENTIMENT

Sentiment indicators attempt to gauge the overall mood of investors. If the sentiment is exuberant, then the market may actually be poised for a correction or perhaps even a bear market. The main reason is that it will get harder and harder to get new buyers into the market.

Headline Indicator

One famous sentiment measure is the "headline indicator." This is when a mainstream magazine—like *Time*—has a front cover story that is extremely bullish. In other words, the masses are rushing into the markets and feel there is little downside.

Secondary Offerings

Another helpful indicator is "secondary offerings." This is when a company sells shares to investors when it is already public. The money from the offering may go to the company—for expansion or to pay down debt—or to existing shareholders, who want to get liquidity. When equity markets are slow or in the bear phase, secondaries are nonexistent. Rather, you see this type of activity when the markets heat up. What's more, the activity gets frothy when markets are near the top.

DEPRESSIONS AND THE STOCK MARKET

The last depression in the United States was from 1929 to 1933. It was a horrible economic event and it was global. In the United States, unemployment hit 25 percent as industrial production plunged by 46 percent and foreign trade collapsed by 70 percent. While the economy recovered somewhat in the middle of the 1930s there was a relapse in 1937. The economy did not get to full employment until the late 1940s. Keep in mind that depressions are quite rare in U.S. history. Yet with the 2007–2008 financial panic, there was some concern that there would be a depression. But with the government's huge stimulus package and the Fed's loose monetary policy, the economy has resumed its growth, albeit at a slow pace.

When it comes to stock prices, it is clear that depressions are the worst. When they occur, many people will lose their wealth and wind up broke. Furthermore, it is likely to take more than a decade to get a real recovery. Given this possibility, it does highlight the importance of having some short-sale elements in a portfolio. It may not be enough to deal with a depression, but it can soften the blow. Or, it may give an investor more time to move assets to liquid alternatives like Treasuries.

Consider that of the two depressions of the past 200 years—1835 to 1842 and 1929 to 1933—there was first a major fall in the stock market. This definitely is reasonable. A major fall in the markets is no fluke and shows a crumbling of the underlying fundamentals of an economy. Also, if the stock fall is large, there will be a "wealth effect." This means that many consumers will feel poorer, even if they had few if little equity holdings. The negative psychology will result in lower spending and lower economic growth for a prolonged period of time.

DETECTING BULL MARKETS

While a bear market is an ideal environment for short sellers, a bull market is just the opposite. This is especially the case in the early and late phases of the bull market, when price appreciation is typically the greatest. The losses can be enormous for short sellers. For example, a bull market can last anywhere from one year to five years, or more. But, the gains can be concentrated in a short period of time, say six months. During these times, the returns can easily be over 50 percent. Consider that the greatest bull market occurred over a three-month period in 1932. The S&P 500 was up a stunning 154.5 percent.

Advance/Decline Indicator

In light of this, it is also important to recognize the emergence of bull markets. One way to gauge this is with the "Advance/Decline Indicator." This is a ratio between the total advances and declines on the New York Stock Exchange (NYSE). The stocks that are unchanged are not included. Since this can be a volatile indicator, one approach is to look at the Advance/Decline Indicator over a period of seven to ten days. If during this time, the ratio is 2:1 or higher, then this is highly positive and a bull market is likely ready to erupt.

Up-Volume Indicator

Along with the Advance/Decline Indicator, you might want to get confirmation from strong volume. You can use the "Up-Volume Indicator." This shows the total number of stocks that are up compared to those that are down (the unchanged stocks are excluded). If the indicator is 9:1 or higher, then the markets are getting bullish.

Of all the strategies in this chapter, perhaps the most important are the Fed indicators. The saying goes that investors should "not fight the Fed." The fact is that this organization has a tremendous impact on liquidity in markets—and can have a major impact on the direction of stock prices, at least in the short term. In the next chapter, we will look at different ways to help position your portfolio with short positions, such as with market-neutral and global macro approaches.

Trading Strategies

Key Concepts

- Looking at different portfolio management approaches
- Analyzing arbitrage
- Understanding quant trading

There are only a few short-only investors. Key reasons include high costs and the risks of short squeezes and buy-ins. Yet short-only investors can generate substantial returns. Consider that Jim Chanos has personally generated hundreds of millions of dollars in trading profits. But his track record has been far from perfect. He has had years where his fund has sustained massive losses. There was even a time when Chanos thought he would not be able to continue with a short-only strategy.

In light of all this, the fact is that it is more common for investors to use a blend of long and short positions. This is the case with a market-neutral portfolio, long-short funds, or quant funds. In fact, these strategies have become significant, especially with the growth of hedge funds over the past 20 years.

MARKET-NEUTRAL PORTFOLIO

A "market-neutral portfolio" attempts to factor out the impact of the overall market. The result should be steady returns, regardless of whether the trend is bullish or bearish.

No doubt, general market and sector declines can have a substantial impact on your portfolio. Keep in mind that during a bear market, it is typical for 90 percent or 95 percent of all stocks to fall in value. This is often known as "correlation risk," since most investments move in the same direction. In such an environment, it can be nearly impossible for even a top-notch stock picker to make money. Interestingly enough, this is where the concept of diversification is misleading. Even if you invest in a broad assortment of stocks and industries, it will not matter in a bear market. Your portfolio will fall. True, the impact may not necessarily be as much as the overall market, but it will probably be close.

Investors also need to be careful with "sector declines." For example, suppose you buy the best company in the semiconductor industry. Again, this may be a moot point. If the semiconductor industry goes into a downtrend phase, your top pick will probably fall too. This sector impact is known as "rotation." And it can be quick and significant. It is not uncommon for a large amount of money to move from one sector to another, resulting in double-digit losses.

Of course, by using a market-neutral strategy, you can generally avoid these problems. This is largely due to simultaneously shorting overvalued stocks and buying undervalued stocks. For example, suppose Boom.com has a P/E ratio of 120 and is clearly overvalued. But XYZ Corp., which is a high-quality software company, is trading at 25 times earnings. You think the valuations of these two companies will eventually converge as investors realize that Boom.com will not grow as fast as expected. At the same time, you think the market is underestimating the potential of XYZ Corp. But for a market-neutral portfolio, you generally need to invest the same amount for both the long and short trade. So you short $10,000 of Boom.com at $125 per share and buy $10,000 of XYZ Corp. at $40.

Let's say that over the next month, Boom.com falls from $125 to $95 or 24 percent and XYZ Corp. climbs to $42 or 5 percent. Your portfolio has gone from $20,000 to $22,900. It's a nice gain.

But here's another possibility: suppose that your long position declined by 5 percent. You still would have a return of $22,400. In other words, if you guess wrong on the market, you may still have a positive return because you are taking a long and short position.

In theory, a market-neutral portfolio is attractive for those investors looking for "absolute returns." Essentially, this means that the portfolio should be positive in any environment. No doubt, a market-neutral portfolio will probably not generate the strong returns of a long-only portfolio (such as in a bull market). But at the same time, there is some downside protection. Yet there are situations when a market-neutral portfolio can be a big problem. This is especially the case during a market mania, when investors keep buying up speculative stocks.

Continuing with our example, suppose that Boom.com continues to surge but the higher-quality stock, XYZ Corp., actually declines. Why? Because it is considered part of the "old economy." This is why a market-neutral strategy did not fare well during the dot-com boom. But this is a rare situation. In a stable environment, a market-neutral strategy can be quite effective. For the most part, it strives to create a portfolio that has a beta of zero. "Beta" represents a portfolio's or stock's volatility compared to a market. If XYZ Corp. has a beta of 1, then it will increase or decrease in the same percentage as the market. A beta of 0.50, on the other hand, will only increase 0.5 percent for every 1 percent increase in the market, and vice versa. But if the beta is zero, then there is no correlation to the market. Instead, to get a return, a portfolio will need to have a positive "alpha." This is a return that is independent of the market. It shows that the investor has good investment selection skills.

A market-neutral sector can work when focusing on a few industries—or even one. It really does not matter. Rather, the key is alpha. And having sector expertise is critical. But an investor still must consider some important points. One is "net exposure." As a portfolio grows, there may be an imbalance of short and long positions. Because of this, a good manager will try to keep the portfolio in equilibrium. If not, then the beta will increase. Next, an investor needs to understand "asset and industry classifications." This means that the paired trade should be for companies that are roughly the same size. After all, investment theory shows that small and large-cap stocks can often diverge. Also, the paired trade should be for similar companies in terms of product line and market focus. For example, a semiconductor company can be quite different from other operators—such as in terms of geography, price points, and so on.

In other words, some industries may be more difficult when pairing a long and short position.

ARBITRAGE

In simple terms, "arbitrage" is when a trader takes advantage of a price discrepancy in two markets. Here's a classic example: the price of gold is $1,000 in London but $980 in New York. A savvy trader would lock in a profit by simultaneously buying gold in New York and shorting the same amount of gold in London. The $20 profit would represent a risk-free 2-percent gain. The premise is that eventually the prices of the two commodities will converge. Actually, it's the impact from arbitrage traders that allows this to happen.

Yet in today's global electronic markets, it is much more difficult to find arbitrage opportunities. Rather, traders will often magnify returns by taking massive positions and using lots of leverage. What's more, there is often the use of sophisticated computer models. The upshot is that an arbitrage opportunity may last just a few seconds—requiring the speed of a computer-based trading system. But such New Age arbitrage systems may not necessarily be risk-free. As seen during 2008, a variety of top funds in this category sustained massive losses.

Despite the risks, arbitrage remains quite popular. The main approaches include statistical arbitrage, merger arbitrage, and convertible arbitrage.

Statistical Arbitrage

Back in the mid-1980s, Gerry Bamberger invented statistical arbitrage. He had a computer science degree from Columbia University and got his start at Morgan Stanley to help develop software for "block trading." These were stock transactions for institutions and were usually for large positions.

Even for a big firm like Morgan Stanley, these trades posed risks. What if it could not sell the securities at a profit, because the market suddenly fell? So Bamberger developed a way to automate paired trades—"statistical arbitrage." This meant that when Morgan Stanley made a block purchase of a stock, it would then short a similar stock. An example would be buying 10,000 shares of United Airlines and then shorting Eastern Airlines. The result should be to lower the volatility in the block trade. But Bamberger realized that block trades actually created a short-term profit opportunity. This was because the trade would temporarily throw the price out of whack. And with sophisticated software, Bamberger could capture the profit. So as Morgan Stanley grew its block-trading business, Bamberger's software was able to juice the returns with statistical arbitrage. It turned out to be a massively successful profit center.

The tough part with statistical arbitrage is to find two securities that have a high degree of correlation. This is ideally 98 percent or so. Of course, this is based on historical trends. But in volatile markets, these relationships can break down and result in unprofitable trades.

Merger Arbitrage

"Merger arbitrage" is when a trader makes a profit from shorting the acquirer's stock and buying the target's shares. This is possible because there is usually a gap in the valuation of the target's current stock price and the buyout price. Why? There are several reasons.

First of all, merger deals can fall apart because of failure to get the necessary shareholder votes or even antitrust approval. Next, a deal may involve more due diligence and the buyer might find negative information that makes the deal unappealing. Another possibility is "adverse market conditions." That is, the financing environment may become extremely difficult or a faltering economy may suddenly deflate the target's business. This is what happened during 2007 to 2008, when a variety of deals unwound. Thus, if a deal does not happen, a merger arbitrage trade could suffer a major loss. The buyer's stock may actually rise and the target's stock may fall.

Interestingly enough, merger arbitrage may also suffer from a lack of deal activity. Keep in mind that mergers often undergo waves, in which several years may see minimal activity. Obviously, in this kind of environment, it is tough to put enough money to work to get good returns.

Convertible Arbitrage

A "convertible bond" is known as a hybrid security. It has a fixed maturity date and interest rate but also allows the investor to convert the instrument into a certain number of common shares. In other words, a convertible bond shares the characteristics of a bond and a common stock. There is even "convertible preferred stock." With this, there is an annual dividend payment that is competitive with a fixed-income instrument, such as a bond. Also, in the event that a company goes into default, a preferred shareholder will get any proceeds before the common shareholders.

But when it comes to convertible arbitrage, the main focus is on convertible bonds. And before looking at an example, it is important to first understand some preliminary concepts.

- **Convertible bonds represent an attractive form of cheap financing for companies:** The reason is that the instrument provides investors with the potential upside from stock appreciation. Because of this, interest rates tend to be lower, especially in light of the company's credit rating. In fact, it is possible that the company may never have to pay back the convertible bond. The reason is that if the stock price rises and investors convert their holdings, the outstanding obligations will go away.
- **A convertible bond is not backed by a company's assets:** Actually, the debts are subordinate to existing debts. So in the event of default, the convertible bond holders will be the last in line to get paid back (at least for debt securities). But this is usually not a big concern for investors. After all, they are looking for the possibility of the upside from the equity. A convertible bond also has a floor on the downside. Suppose the value of the underlying stock of a convertible bond plunges. Will the value fall off the convertible bond by the same amount? Most likely it will not. This is because the interest payments will act as a support on the value of the bond.

- **A convertible bond may be callable:** This means that the company has the right to repurchase the security. Granted, this may be at a 5-percent to 10-percent premium to the face value. But this often acts as a ceiling on the value.

To see how convertible bonds work, here's an example: XYZ Corp. issues $100 million in convertible bonds. The coupon rate is 4 percent and the investors have a right to convert the bond into common stock at $20 per share. With a $1,000 face value, an investor can convert each bond into 50 shares. Why not convert now? Well, the current stock price of XYZ Corp. is $15. So to convert at this point, the investor will only get $750 in value for the common shares (50 shares times $15 per share). This is called the "conversion value." But over time, suppose the stock price rises above $20. If so, an investor may want to consider converting the bond into common shares. Or, over the life of the bond, if the stock price remains at the conversion price or lower, then it may make sense to wait to get the principal back at maturity. There are also times when there are discrepancies between the price of the convertible bond and the common stock. The upshot is an arbitrage opportunity.

To continue with the example, suppose that the convertible bond is trading at $850 but the stock price is $18. This means that the conversion value is at $900 ($18 times 50 shares). With this, an arbitrage trade would involve buying the convertible bond and shorting 50 shares of the common stock. Next, you can then turn the convertible bond into 50 shares and use this to cover your short. You will then have made a $50 profit.

Interestingly enough, there is often a difference between the value of a convertible bond and the equivalent common stock. But the amounts are usually too small to make a profit—especially when transaction costs are factored in. But yes, there are cases when the valuations diverge, which often happens when markets are highly volatile.

GLOBAL MACRO

"Global macro" is when an investor focuses mostly on major economic moves, such as inflation, gross domestic product (GDP), and so on. There is also analysis of geopolitical events like wars and protectionism. In terms of investments, the plays are usually major short or long positions in currencies, swaps, and interest rate futures. These markets have lots of liquidity and allow for large amounts of leverage. So, even a small move can mean substantial returns.

This also means there can be significant risks. For example, even top-notch global macro players like George Soros have sustained massive losses on their trades. But keep in mind that a variety of global macro funds performed well during 2008. After all, they were alerted to the impending troubles in the global economy and made short trades to capitalize on the situation.

QUANT TRADING

"Quant trading" uses superfast computers to run highly complicated mathematical algorithms. These are based on many types of market data, in which the goal is to find patterns and trends. The profit opportunities may be fairly small and not last long—which is why computers are required. Quant funds often use heavy amounts of leverage to magnify these returns. But as seen during 2008 to 2010, the strategies can wind up resulting in significant losses. In fact, a variety of top funds had to shut down.

Quant funds may not necessarily have many traditional investment professionals. The employees may be computer programmers, mathematicians, and even physicists. Obviously, such high-caliber people are hard to find—and require large compensation packages.

The origins of quant funds actually go back to the early 1970s, with the pioneering efforts of Ed Thorp. He started his career as a mathematics professor but wanted to see if his equations could generate income. His first target was blackjack, in which he tested various strategies using an IBM 704 computer. He realized that a blackjack player had an edge by using card-counting techniques and based on the fact that the cards were not reshuffled after every deal. Based on this work, he wrote a highly popular book: *Beat the Dealer*. It became an instant best-seller and Thorp turned into a celebrity. After awhile, Thorp was becoming a problem for casinos, who wanted to blacklist him. So he moved on to a much bigger casino: Wall Street.

While he understood the principles of the efficient market hypothesis, he thought there were holes in the theory. The place he studied was "warrants." These are similar to options, in which the buyer gets the right to buy a stock at a certain price (but a warrant usually lasts longer than an option, say ten years or more). Thorp tried to find mispricings in the warrant and the underlying stock, which could mean easy, risk-free profits.

The problem was that warrants required the prediction of stock prices, which was no easy task. But Thorp used his mathematical skills and computer knowledge to create pricing models. Over time, he found there were indeed profit-making opportunities and his approach became known as convertible arbitrage. Thorp even wrote a book about it: *Beat the Market*. Yet again, he had another best-seller, which also became a classic for the quant industry.

He started the first quant fund in 1969, which turned out to be a huge success. For over two decades, he posted positive returns despite the terrible bear market of 1973 to 1974, as well as the stock market crash of 1987. Like any successful investment strategy, Thorp's quant fund got much attention. Increasingly, Wall Street firms started to develop their own funds so as to benefit from the growing profits. But it was not until the 1990s that quant funds became a powerful force. Some of the key players entered the scene, including Ken Griffin (Citadel Investment Group), Peter Muller (Morgan Stanley's PDT fund), Cliff Asness (AQR Capital Management), Boaz Weinstein (Deutsche Bank), and Jim Simons (Renaissance Technologies).

These well-known quant funds would consistently generate market-beating results and attracted huge amounts of assets. In some cases, the funds exceeded $30 billion. But were these returns mostly because of the bull market and high levels of liquidity? What would happen if the markets fell or underwent extreme volatility? Would the computer strategies work then? For the most part, these were theoretical questions. But of course, the quant funds said that such events were infrequent and the computers would be fast enough to deal with these adverse events.

However, there were some early problems. The first major event came from Long-Term Capital Management (LTCM). Started in 1994, the fund had a top-notch team that included the Nobel Prize winners Myron Scholes and Robert Merton, the team that created the model for pricing options. The fund used quant strategies that generated huge profits. The returns came to the following:

Long-Term Capital Management Returns

1994	28%
1995	43%
1996	41%
1997	17%

But the models did not account for low-probability events, such as Russia's default on its sovereign debt. As a result, LTCM suffered tremendous losses, especially with the extreme levels of borrowed money. Because of this, LTCM collapsed in 1998 and Federal Reserve Chairman Alan Greenspan orchestrated a bailout with major Wall Street firms providing the capital. The irony is that the quant funds got a boost from this event.

Quant Funds and the Credit Default Swap

Because of the flight to safety, major investors started to look at credit derivatives. In theory, these were meant to protect bond investments in the event of a default.

For example, suppose XYZ Corp. wanted to issue $100 million in bonds. But there was some concern from investors about the long-term ability of the company to meet the obligations. One idea was to create a "credit default swap (CDS)," essentially, an insurance policy that would pay investors $100 million if XYZ Corp. defaults.

A CDS would have an annual premium—again, like an insurance policy, which could last for five years or so. Also, the CDS was a "structured product." This meant that buyers and sellers had to negotiate over a long period of time—which could easily last a month—to put together the CDS. In the middle of the transaction was usually an investment bank, like Goldman Sachs and Morgan Stanley. Once a CDS was created, it would then trade on the "Over-the-Counter market." This has little regulation and is really just a group of brokers from different investment banks that place trades for clients.

All in all, a credit default swap looked like a conservative product. And yes, quant funds saw a huge opportunity to trade them. In fact, it would be an effective way to short a company. The reason is that if a company has troubles, the prices on its CDSs would increase because of the higher risk of default. The CDS trades would also result in more short selling of typical equities.

For example, suppose a major investment bank agrees to write a CDS on XYZ Corp.'s debt. What if XYZ Corp. actually defaults on the loan? In this case, the investment bank would have to pay off the holder of the CDS. To hedge this risk, the investment bank would actually short shares in XYZ Corp., so as to hedge the position. When done on a massive basis, this type of trading would wind up creating substantial risks in the financial markets and was a big part of the plunge in the markets in 2007 to 2008.

Other Factors Influencing the Success of Quant Funds

Besides the emergence of the CDS market, there were some other important drivers for the success of quant funds. Of course, one was "high-frequency trading (HFT)," which uses high-powered computers to place quick trades.

Another important factor was the "carry trade." After the crash in the late 1980s and the ensuing slow economy, the interest rates in Japan remained at mostly 1 percent. Quant funds—and many other funds—saw an opportunity to make a risk-free trade. This would involve borrowing money in yen at a rock-bottom rate and investing the capital in higher-yield investments in other countries. Of course, quant funds used heavy amounts of leverage to amplify these trades.

Even the emergence of the "Bloomberg terminal" was critical to the growth of quant funds. The technology allowed real-time access to many types of alternative investments across the globe. With this information, quant funds were able to devise more sophisticated models. For example, a quant fund would measure the price-to-book value of the U.S. stock market and also other stock markets, such as in Europe and Asia. If there were differences in value, a quant fund would short the more expensive market and buy the cheaper one. From there, a quant fund would apply these to other asset classes like currencies, commodities, and so on. Think of this as global arbitrage.

THE FALL OF THE QUANTS

From 2000 to 2007, quant funds enjoyed a surge in earnings from the investments in structured products. A key one was the "collateralized debt obligation (CDO)." A typical CDO would contain various types of mortgage loans, with different levels of default risk. These were known as "tranches." One tranche would be a high-quality one, with a credit rating of AAA and so on. This created a perception of safety and made it easier for conservative financial institutions to buy CDOs. But the credit ratings were far from foolproof. For example, the long-term prices in real estate appeared to be fairly stable, at least on a national level. But in light of the speculation in the markets, would things be different this time?

One trend was an increase in "subprime loans." These mortgage loans were for people who did not have to provide much, or any, verification of income. This was certainly a new phenomenon on Wall Street. Yet the computer models from the credit agencies did not make any significant adjustments. But what if most or all the loans were bad and the defaults skyrocketed? In this case, a AAA tranche would go to zero. And yes, this happened to many CDOs. Financial firms like Lehman Brothers and Merrill Lynch wound up with billions in illiquid CDOs.

Another problem is that the quant funds also did not account for this adverse event. Their strategy was to stick to a "relative value approach" when trading CDOs. This would mean shorting the overvalued ones and buying the cheap issues. Of course, this strategy came apart when the values on CDOs evaporated. Thus, in 2007, two major Bear Stearns hedge funds—which invested heavily in CDOs—had to be shut down. This eventually led to the failure of the investment bank.

While subprime loans were a relatively small part of the financial system, the distress in this asset class spread to others. The main reason is that CDO funds were part of larger financial complexes. So, to make up for the losses, they would then need to find liquidity quickly. This meant selling quality assets, such as blue-chip stocks. For example, shares in companies like Disney and Kraft would suddenly fall. At the same time, lower-quality stocks shot up in value. Needless to say, this made statistical arbitrage strategies lose money. As a result, these funds also had to sell off quality assets and close the short positions in their lower-quality positions, which meant buying the stocks. This turned into a vicious cycle and resulted in a plunge in the markets.

There was yet another problem: In September 2008, the Securities and Exchange Commission (SEC) banned short selling on roughly 800 financial services firms. The goal was to help prevent the meltdown in equities. Thus, for the many quant funds that had short positions on financial services firms, the results were catastrophic. The values of these companies immediately had a rally. It was not uncommon for some stocks to increase over 100 percent in a short period of time.

Perhaps the biggest flaw in the quant funds is that it failed to account for human nature. Mathematics and physics can certainly predict things like the movement of planets and planes. But how effective can these approaches deal with human-driven activities, such as trading? After all, there were many smart people who invested in companies like Pets.com, even though there were no clear business models.

It should be no surprise that—over the years—academia has been evolving a new type of theory, called "behavioral finance." The discipline tries to factor in the intricacies of human behavior. In fact, it is not uncommon for smart people to make irrational financial decisions, which certainly makes it difficult for mathematical models to deal with.

THE GREATEST TRADE EVER

Before 2007, John Paulson was considered a has-been hedge fund manager. While he had a strong performance record, he was not having much success attracting large amounts of money. Perhaps a part of this was that Paulson used traditional fundamental analysis, not high-powered computers, to pull off his trades.

Regardless, Paulson thought the quant funds—as well as many other hedge funds—were in trouble. They were investing in the huge real estate market, which was undergoing massive appreciation. Paulson believed the bubble would eventually burst, so he spent roughly two years researching the real estate market, which involved hiring experts, buying databases, and attending conferences. He was building his investment thesis—the trigger for why the market would fall.

But he had a big problem: how do you short real estate? There was no direct way of doing this. So Paulson had to get creative and this involved purchasing credit default swaps (CDSs) on collateralized debt obligations (CDOs). It took lots of work, since these instruments were highly complicated and involved hundreds of pages of disclosures. But each CDS would have two sides. The seller of this contract believed that CDOs would not go bust. Of course, the buyer thought just the opposite. All in all, these CDS arrangements involved two sophisticated investors betting against each other.

Unlike other investors at the time, Paulson did not use borrowed money to make his trades. He believed this was too risky. Over time, leverage can eat into returns. But then again, Paulson's investments in CDSs were already a form of leverage. These instruments would skyrocket if the underlying value of the assets fell. Over the next two years, he would become a superstar. In fact, he struck the biggest trade in the history of Wall Street. From 2007 to 2008, he made $6 billion in profits—for himself.

In this chapter, we have covered mostly sophisticated trading strategies. These are really for full-time investors who work on Wall Street, not individual investors. But it is possible to participate in these approaches with mutual funds and hedge funds. But as seen with quant funds, there are risks and you need to do some research before making an investment decision. In the next section, we will take a look at using options when shorting. Again, so long as you understand the risks—and manage them effectively—options can be quite profitable.

CHAPTER 12

Shorting with Options

Key Concepts

- Options versus short selling
- Straddles and spreads
- Index options
- Tax issues

An option is known as a derivative because the valuation depends on an underlying asset. This type of investment has been around for hundreds of years, going back to the early stock exchanges in Holland and London. But the modern options market got its start in 1973, with the creation of the Chicago Board Options Exchange (CBOE). The organization standardized the marketplace, which led to increased liquidity and trading. Now the exchange has options on over 2,200 companies, 22 stock indexes, and 150 exchange-traded funds (ETFs).

The options markets has been a strong growth segment over the years. From 1999 to 2009, annual volume for equity option trading has spiked from 400 million to 3.5 billion. Some of the reasons include the emergence of electronic markets and the Internet, the ease of trading from online brokers, and more education. Options are also popular because they provide short sellers with an alternative for making their trades. In fact, these instruments are highly effective in developing sophisticated strategies and hedges. At the same time, options are much cheaper now. The commissions are comparable to a regular stock trades.

THE BASICS OF OPTIONS

An "option" gives you the right—but not the obligation—to buy 100 shares at a fixed price for a certain period of time (which often ranges from one quarter to one year). This is also known as a "call option." There is also another type of option: a "put option." This gives you the right to sell 100 shares at a fixed price—called "the exercise price"—for a certain period of time. For both a call option and a put option, you will pay "a premium." So your total investment is the premium price times 100 shares.

Whether you buy a call option or a put option, it means that you are making a judgment on the direction of a stock or other security. With a call option, you believe the value will increase and with a put option, you think the opposite will occur.

To understand this, let's take an example of a put option. Suppose that you think XYZ Corp., which is trading at $35, is overvalued. You go to your computer and find the quote shown in Table 12-1 for a put option.

TABLE 12-1

Put Option Chain

Strike Price	Contract Name	Last Trade	Change	Bid	Ask	Volume	Interest
33.00	XYZ\11M22\33.0	1.90	0.16	1.85	1.91	754	4,507
34.00	XYZ\11M22\34.0	2.25	0.21	2.25	2.32	256	10,345
35.00	XYZ\11M22\35.0	2.74	0.21	2.72	2.85	512	28,270
36.00	XYZ\11M22\36.0	3.30	0.40	3.30	3.45	498	5,803
37.00	XYZ\11M22\37.0	3.90	0.15	3.90	4.10	245	3,786

This is an "option chain," which shows the contracts available for a list of strike prices (shown in Column One), which will never change. The expiration of the options is in January and the current month is September. Column Two shows the unique identifier for the contract and Column Three shows the most recent trade. As you can see by the next column, the put option has increased in value over the last trading day. The last two columns show the activity in each put option. The "Volume" is the number of purchases of the option and the "Interest" shows the outstanding open contracts. These are option purchases that have not been exercised.

To pull off your trade, you want to buy the XYZ Corp. option that has a strike price of $35. To do this, you will pay the "Ask" price or $285 ($2.85 times 100). This is the premium and is the only amount you will need to pay. There are no margin requirements. Since this is an official contract, there is another party to this transaction. In this case, this person is the seller of the put option. He or she will agree to purchase the 100 shares you have.

What if this party fails to deliver? An options exchange has the "Options Clearing Corporation (OCC)." This organization keeps track of all the options contracts. What's more, the OCC will be the initial seller of your put option and will then connect this transaction to a put seller. The organization will also guarantee the exercise of the put option. This is a form of insurance, which provides confidence in options trading. In other words, there is no need to be worried that the contract will be fulfilled.

A put option will also provide the short seller with "leverage." This means that he or she will only have to put up a fraction of the total amount of the securities involved. In the put option trade at a $35 strike price, the total amount is $3,500. But of course, the short seller only had to pay $285. This means that a small change in XYZ Corp.'s stock price can have a significant impact on the premium.

Let's take a look at several scenarios. First, suppose the stock price of XYZ Corp. falls from $35 to $29 in the next two weeks. Your put option now has intrinsic value and is considered to be "in-the-money." This is the difference between the strike price and the current stock price—which is $6 ($35 minus $29). But the premium on your option is likely to be higher than $6. The reason is that an option will also have "time value." This accounts for the possibility that the stock may fall even more and generate more value for the option.

When you originally bought the put option, the premium was $285. This was all time value (since the strike price and the stock price were the same). But time value will decrease over time. In fact, this will accelerate as the option gets close to the expiration. Simply put, there will not be much time for the stock to move. So if the stock price remains at $35 and there is only one week left until expiration, the premium may be pennies on the dollar. Unless the stock falls by $3, you will lose your $285 investment. Or, suppose the stock falls by $1 during this time. Your premium value will be $1 and you will have taken a big loss on your trade.

Because of the problems with time value, some investors will use options with longer expiration terms. These are known as "long-term equity anticipation securities (LEAPs)." These are identical to listed options except the expiration can run from one to three years. Yet this still may not be enough time for some stocks to fall enough. Besides, because of the extra time allowed, LEAPs will probably be fairly expensive, making it more difficult to put on profitable trades.

Aside from the introduction of LEAPs, options markets have changed in other important ways. Originally, investors could only buy "listed options," which have standardized terms. But over the years, the options exchanges have allowed customization of con-tracts—known as "structured options." This is done using "flexible exchange (FLEX) options." Within certain parameters, you can change the exercise price and the expiration. Yet these are still mostly for sophisticated investors.

While all these innovations are helpful, they can add com-plexity and risks. As seen in these examples, a $6 drop in the value of XYZ Corp. can double the value of your put option. But at the same time, a price that fails to move will mean that you lose every-thing. All in all, this shows the real impact of leverage.

Investors need to be careful in dealing with the risks of options. It is not uncommon for a beginner to quickly lose his or her nest egg with options. Because of this, a brokerage firm is required to be proactive in determining if options trading is appropriate for an investor. This involves filling out a form that gauges risk toler-ance. There will also be brochures that explain options trading. Finally, even if a broker approves an account, there may still be lim-itations, such as in terms of the types of strategies allowed and the investment limits.

Despite all this, short sellers see put options as an effective trading technique. Consider that this has no buy-in, no requirement to find shares to borrow, and no need to pay dividends to the lender of the shares. However, there are some instances where a put option does not work. This would obviously be the case when a security does not have a put option. Next, even if a put option is trading, the volume may be light. As a result, the cost of buying the put could be too expensive. This could also be the result of high volatility in the underlying security as investors want to protect themselves. From time to time—especially in volatile markets—the premiums can be extremely expensive.

OPTION WRITING

Generally, the buyer of a call option or a put option is speculating on the price of the underlying security. But on the other side of the transaction, the option writer is usually taking a more conservative approach. He or she will get the premium from the option buyer, which can be a nice return.

Perhaps the most conservative approach is the "covered call." Interestingly enough, this is really a form of short selling. In this transaction, the call writer owns shares that he or she believes will either stay at the same price or fall. But the investor does not want to sell the shares yet. For example, suppose you own 100 shares of XYZ Corp., which are currently trading at $35. You purchased the shares at $15 two years ago. You decide to write one call option against XYZ Corp. that has an exercise price of $2. For this, you get a premium of $200. Suppose that within three months, the stock falls to $34. Since the call buyer will not exercise the option, you will get to keep the $200 premium. After this, you may decide to write another call option against XYZ Corp. Keep in mind that this ongoing call writing is a popular strategy to generate income, so long as the stock is fairly stable. An additional benefit would be if the stock has a strong dividend.

The call writer does not have to wait until expiration to close out the transaction. For example, suppose that your XYZ Corp. call is only trading at 20 cents because of the fall in the stock price. You can buy a call to cancel your option position. And yes, you may then decide to write another call to generate more income. One of the problems of call writing, however, is that you miss out on surges in the stock price. Let's say that XYZ Corp. goes to $40 per share. The call buyer will probably exercise the option (the chances of this increase as the option gets closer to expiration). In this scenario, you will get to keep the $200 premium. However, you will have to sell your shares at $35 and miss out on an additional $5 per-share profit.

THE RISKS OF CALL WRITING

While covered call writing tends to be conservative, there are some risks. Perhaps the most important is when an investor selects an option *only* because of the high premium. The problem is that the premium is usually high because the stock has lots of volatility. In other words, the investor may be purchasing high-risk stocks. The result could either be a major decline in the stock price—or a surge. So call writers will tend to stick with larger companies, which are more stable.

A way to gauge risk levels is to look at the so-called Greeks. And yes, these are indicators that have Greek symbols. A key one is the "beta." This shows the relationship between a stock's price and the overall market. If the beta is over 1.0, then the stock will generally move higher or lower than the relevant benchmark. The result is that the premiums should be higher—but so will the risk. Next, there is the "delta." This shows the relationship in movements between an option and the underlying stock. If the delta is 1.0, then the relationship is the same. If the delta starts to increase, this shows more volatility in the option and a higher risk level.

Why? It could be because investors have insider information. For example, some traders may know that the company will be taken over, which would result in a much higher stock price. No doubt, this would be a terrible time for an investor to short stocks. So be careful if there are sudden spikes in call option activity—especially at higher exercise prices.

There is also another risk to call writing—when an investor writes "naked calls." This is the same as a covered call, except that the writer does not own the shares. For the most part, this is a short position.

For example, suppose XYZ Corp. is selling for $10 per share and you write a call against this for 100 shares. The strike price is $12 and the premium is $2. Thus, you get $200. If the stock price remains at $12 or falls, then the option will become worthless and you can pocket the $200 premium. Of course, the reverse can also happen. In fact, if the stock price surges—such as to $15 or higher—then you will need to pay a substantial amount to meet your obligation of the naked call. Like a short-sale transaction, you face the possibility of "unlimited" losses. Needless to say, naked call writing is highly risky and should be used with caution. Because of this, you are required to set up a margin account. The reason is that if a trade takes on increasing losses, the brokerage firm will want the investor to put up more money. If not, the broker will unwind the position.

SHORT-SALE PROTECTION

One of the biggest risks of a short position is a sudden surge in the stock price (as seen earlier with the takeover example). But the use of a deep out-of-the-money call can act as insurance against this.

Let's take an example. Several months ago, you shorted 100 shares of XYZ Corp. at $30. Now the shares are trading at $25. But you think there is further downside on the stock. Yet you still want some level of protection. In this case, you buy a call that has an exercise price of $27. Since it is "out-of-the-money," the premium is 75 cents or $75. Next, suppose the stock price of XYZ Corp. goes back to $30. Of course, you will have lost all your gains on the short sale. However, your call option will be "in-the-money" by $3, so you can sell your option for $300. Or suppose XYZ Corp. goes to $40 because of a buyout offer. Again, your call option will be highly profitable and essentially eliminate the "unlimited risk" of your short position.

MARRIED PUT

To protect a gain in a stock, an investor can short "against the box." This simply means shorting the stock at the current price. The result is that the gain will be locked in despite the movement in the stock. You can also do this using a put option. This strategy is called a "married put." Suppose you purchased XYZ Corp. at $20 and it quickly rises to $30. You want to hold onto the stock but think the market may have some volatility in the short term. So you buy a put option with an exercise price of $20 for $2 a share.

One possibility is that the stock price increases—or even stays the same. Keep in mind that the put option only has time value. So if the stock stays at $20 or increases in price, the premium will decline and hit zero at expiration. You will have lost the $2 premium and your gain in the stock would be $8, not $10.

Now let's say the stock price falls. When this happens, the put option will go into the money and have intrinsic value. In general, every dollar decline will increase the option value by $1. If the option declines up to $2, your option will offset much of the decline in your stock option. But you may decide to buy the option before expiration, which is likely to be at a premium that is pennies on the dollar.

However, a married put may have a tax consequence. The IRS may consider this to be essentially the sale of the stock. If so, you would owe the capital gains taxes on the $10 profit on the stock. This is definitely something that requires the assistance of a tax expert.

STRADDLE

A "straddle" is the simultaneous purchase and sale of the same number of calls or puts, which have the same strike prices and expiration prices. The idea is that profits are based on the size of the price movements—not whether they increase or decrease.

One variation is a "long straddle." Despite its name, it actually is an interesting strategy for short sellers. Suppose you think XYZ Corp., a biotech company, will not get its drug approved. This would mean a huge plunge in the stock price. However, what if the Food and Drug Administration (FDA) does approve the drug? In this case, the stock will spike. So a long straddle is built to be profitable if there is a big move on the upside or the downside. It means buying call and put options at the same exercise price.

As an example, suppose that XYZ Corp. stock is at $40 per share. The put has a premium of $3 and the call has a premium of $2. To break even, it will need to create $5 in intrinsic value.

As you can see, the strategy is expensive. But if you think there will likely be a big move in the stock price, a long straddle will certainly be an effective strategy.

THE BEAR SPREAD AND
THE PUT BACK SPREAD

With a "spread," you will use two options contracts with either a different strike price or expiration date, or both. The goal is to make money on gaps in the market. But it can also be used to profit from downward moves—called a "bear spread." There are several variations on this strategy. First, you can do the following close to the market price of the stock, in which case you will sell an "at-the-money" call and buy an out-of-the-money call.

To understand this, let's take an example. XYZ Corp. is selling at $50 per share and you think the price will fall a couple of dollars during the next three months. You buy a call with a strike price of $52, which has a premium of $1. You then write a call with a strike price at $50, which nets you a premium of $1. The result is that you have a credit spread of $1 or $100. Assuming you are correct about the direction of the stock, this will be your maximum profit in the trade. That is, if the stock stays at $50 or goes lower, both calls will expire worthless and you keep the $200 premium. Or, if the stock rises above $50, you will lose your net credit amount of $100.

Another approach is to use a "bear spread with put options." Like the example above, you will focus on options at or near the current market price. This means buying an "at-the-money" put and then writing an "out-of-the-money" put. Let's continue with the XYZ Corp. example. In this situation, you will buy a put with an exercise price at $52, which has a premium of $1. Then you will sell a put at $50 and get a premium of $2. Again, your net credit spread is $1, which is your maximum profit.

A short seller may also try another interesting spread: the "put back spread," which you would implement when you believe there will be a major decline in the stock price. In general, the trade involves selling a put at a higher strike price and then buying a larger number of puts at a lower strike price. The goal is to make this trade with a low-debit balance (which is your net cash outlay). Although, in some cases it may even be possible to get a positive credit spread.

The focus on in-the-money puts is important since these tend to have a higher probability of being profitable. At the same time, the sale of the put should provide some downside protection—so long as the stock price does not surge.

INDEX OPTIONS

As the name implies, an "index option" allows an investor to use puts and calls for a variety of benchmarks. One of the most popular ones is the Dow Jones Industrial Average (DJIA). This is the oldest benchmark and it tracks 30 of some of the top companies in the United States, like IBM, Wal-Mart, and Johnson & Johnson.

The DJIA is a simple average. This means adding up the stock prices and dividing it by 30. However, because of stock splits and mergers, the divisor has had to be adjusted over the years. It is currently 0.13532775. Because of this calculation, the DJIA is highly sensitive to moves in a company's stock price, especially for higher priced stocks. So a drop in a couple of stocks can have an exaggerated impact on the index.

Next, there is the S&P 500. This includes 500 top companies from the New York Stock Exchange (NYSE) and the Nasdaq. While the index tries to diversify across industries this may not always be the case. For example, during the dot-com boom, the tech stocks grew to a major percentage of the S&P 500. This also happened to the financial stocks from 2002 to 2007. The S&P 500 is market weighted. This means that the change in each stock is based on its market capitalization. So a large company like Microsoft will have a much bigger impact on the index than a mid-cap stock.

A major advantage of using an index option is that the volatility tends to be lower than for options on individual stocks. The reason is that an index has diversification and the swings are usually muted. Of course, there are certain times—such as when there are financial panics—when the volatility can be extreme. After all, the Dow fell 22 percent during the crash of 1987. Also, index options have several differences when compared to individual stock options. For example, index options have cash settlements. So at the time of expiration, the seller of the option does not have to deliver all the stocks in the index. Instead, he or she will settle the contract with a cash payment. Next, the size of the option may vary. In general, the value of an option is the index multiplied by $100. But again, some index options will have a different multiplier.

Another difference is on the exercise. While many index options allow the investor to buy or sell an option before expiration, there are some that only allow this at certain time periods. In other words, it is important to research the option before making a purchase. The terms can certainly have a major impact on the investment.

For the most part, you can use the same strategies with index options that are covered earlier in this chapter. For example, if you think the market will fall, you may decide to write a call against the S&P 500. But, this is likely to be a naked call—unless you own the equivalent 500 stocks, which would actually be tough to do. True, some sophisticated hedge funds and quant funds can do this, but it is usually not for the individual investor. Or, the investor can purchase a put against the S&P 500, which is much easier. But again, these options tend to be efficiently priced and often expire worthless. So even though there tends to be less risk with index options, an investor still needs to be very cautious.

PAPER TRADING

While options are an effective strategy for short sellers, the fact remains that the process is far from easy. As seen in this chapter, options allow for high-end strategies. But if done incorrectly, the risks can be substantial. Because of this, it is important to get training. In fact, there are a variety of options schools and training programs in the United States. If you are serious about this type of investing, it is probably worth considering.

Another idea is to use "paper trading." This is where you sign up for a Web-based system that simulates options trading. In most cases, they are based on actual market information. This paper-trading approach is extremely effective in learning the fundamentals of options trading—and should prepare you for success.

Finally, even when you have a good grasp of options trading, it is smart to use discipline and planning in all your trades. This means looking at the possible outcomes of your strategies and at what stock prices you will make and lose money. You can do this using an Excel spreadsheet.

TAXES

When it comes to stock options, the tax implications can get extremely complicated, especially when an investor uses strategies like spreads, straddles, and so on. It is definitely a good idea to seek out a tax professional who understands the rules.

But there are some general principles to keep in mind. First of all, with the purchase or writing of a put or call option, there is no gain or loss recognized. Instead, this happens when the option is exercised. The trade may be subject to either a lower capital gains rate (if held for over a year) or ordinary rates (if held for less than a year). However, since most options expire within less than a year, you will likely face short-term gains or losses.

Another important rule is "the wash sale." If you buy shares in a stock and then within 30 days buy a stock option—which produces a loss—then you will not be able to recognize this loss. The tax law discourages short-term trading, which is meant only to generate offsetting losses to lower the tax bite.

For many investors, the belief is that options are too risky. While this is the case with buying puts on speculative stocks—as well as various other strategies—the fact remains that options trading can be low risk. This is certainly the case with covered call writing. But of course, you need to have a strong understanding of the strategies, which does take some time. In the next chapter, we will look at another interesting topic: shorting commodities. Over the past decade, there has been much interest in this category, which is likely to continue for some time.

CHAPTER 13

Shorting Commodities

Key Concepts

- Understanding the drivers of commodities
- How to use futures contracts to short commodities
- Looking at the main commodities, like oil and gold

A "financial asset" is something that is intangible, like a stock or a bond. There are also "real assets," which include land, commercial properties, homes, and commodities. Hedge funds and other sophisticated investors have historically focused on financial assets. These are fairly liquid and have proven to be effective for developing portfolios. But these investors also realize that there are lucrative opportunities in real assets.

A key reason for this is "correlation." This shows the relationship between one asset class to another. If it is 1-to-1, then an investment does not provide any diversification. After all, the purpose of diversification is to lower risk. As one asset class goes down, another asset class should increase in value. As for real assets, there is often little correlation with financial assets. In fact, with futures and the emergence of exchange-traded funds (ETFs), it is much easier for investors to short the commodities asset class.

A LOOK AT COMMODITIES

"Commodities" are unique investments because they represent assets like sugar, oil, hogs, copper, and wheat that are essential for the lives of everyone. Because of this, it is nearly impossible for a commodity to fall to zero, as it should always have at least some value. Yet commodities experience volatility in prices for reasons including bad weather and even war. Another reason that commodities are so distinctive is that all commodities within a given subcategory will have the same value. So if you have wheat, you do not have to worry about its version or type. In this sense, a commodity is interchangeable (unless it has been tampered with). Because of this, investors only need to worry about the supply and demand of the commodity. But you can divide commodities into certain categories.

- **Metals:** They have two subcategories. There are precious metals, which include gold, platinum, and silver. Then there are industrial base metals, which include aluminum, copper, lead, nickel, palladium, tin, and zinc.
- **Energy:** This comes mostly from fossil fuels and includes commodities like coal, crude oil, heating oil, and natural gas.
- **Livestock:** This includes feeder cattle, lean hogs, live cattle, and pork bellies. These commodities have become more important over the years because they are critical for economic development of emerging economies like China and India (as their diets move toward more protein).
- **Agricultural industry commodities:** This includes grains and oil seeds like corn, soybeans, and wheat. There are also soft ones, such as cocoa, coffee, cotton, orange juice, and sugar.
- **Commodities that do not fit the traditional definition:** This includes ethanol, emission allowance credits, and interest rates.

As you research commodities, you will realize that there are many helpful resources. Some Web sites include the U.S. Geological Survey, the American Bureau of Metal Statistics, and the American Metal Market. You can also find good information on the

Web sites for the various commodities exchanges like the COMEX, the Chicago Mercantile Exchange, and the Chicago Board of Trade.

For short sellers, there is often focus on the main commodities. The top ones include oil, natural gas, gold, aluminum, and copper.

OIL

Some short sellers have made huge amounts of money from oil. Consider the Gulf War of 1990. While it was clear the United States would attack Iraq, it was far from certain what would be the impact on oil. But the price of oil was steadily increasing as the start of the war got closer. So, several hedge funds bought oil futures to benefit from this trend. But they thought that the war would end quickly and that prices would fall. To this end, they started shorting the oil futures. It turned out to be a lucrative strategy. It also points out how investment strategies can be controversial. Some think it is unseemly to make profits from wars. But when looking at the history of investments, this is quite common. Take a look at Nathan Mayer Rothschild, who had advance information that Napoleon lost the Battle of Waterloo. He was able to make a fortune from the trade.

As for oil, it should continue to be a good source of opportunities for short sellers—at least in terms of short-term moves. However, there still needs to be some caution. It is reasonable to assume that the price of oil is likely to increase over the next couple of decades. The fact is that it is getting tougher to find new sources of oil—at least in large amounts that make a difference in terms of the global demand, which is 87 barrels a day (for 2010). Of course, U.S. oil production peaked in the 1970s. What's more, key oil fields across the world have also peaked, such as in Alaska and the North Sea.

The wild card in oil is Saudi Arabia. The problem is that the government is secretive about its reserves. However, there are some analysts who believe that the Saudi oil fields have peaked or are close to doing so. If this is the case, it likely means that there will be constraints on oil supply, which should mean strong long-term price increases. Thus, for short sellers, oil may not be a good bet. But oil can be a helpful indicator for short sellers. When oil prices reach high levels, the global economy will start to slow down. Oil is a pervasive component for virtually everything. For example, the skyrocketing oil prices of 2008 were clearly a key reason for the global recession.

NATURAL GAS

Natural gas is a vital commodity for things like electricity production in the United States. In fact, it may play an important role in other areas, such as fuel for autos. Despite all this, natural gas shows how new technologies can have a big impact on supply. Because of drilling innovations, it has become possible for producers to extract natural gas from areas that were once considered too costly. As a result, a large amount of supply came onto the market between 2007 to 2009, causing a big drop in natural gas prices.

The upshot was that some top-notch investors sustained large losses. A prime example is Amaranth Advisors, which had about $10 billion in assets. The firm started in convertible arbitrage but eventually became a big player in energy futures, with a focus on natural gas. The problem is that Amaranth had little internal risk controls and allowed one of its young traders to make a massive directional bet. Within a week, the fund lost $5 billion and eventually had to be closed down.

GOLD

As a commodity, gold is not necessarily essential. It is mostly for luxury items, which is a fairly niche market. But this does not matter for many investors. For centuries, gold has been the linchpin of currencies. This was through the gold standard, which made it possible to trade paper money for the precious metal. Yet the United States went off the gold standard during the 1930s. In fact, this happened in most developed countries. A big problem was that—as economies became unstable—there was a rush to convert paper money. But this would jeopardize the U.S. gold supply.

Then, after World War II, there was a need to establish a stable foreign currency system. To this end, the United States used the dollar for this purpose and it was actually backed by gold. At the time, the conversion of gold was $35 per ounce. The currency system worked until the early 1970s, when inflation started to emerge and there was a loss of confidence in the U.S. dollar. President Nixon then made the decision to allow currencies to be freely traded. At the same time, it was also possible for Americans to buy and sell gold (this had been outlawed during the Great Depression). As inflation continued to increase, the price of gold also rose. The price of gold reached about $850 an ounce in the late 1970s. But after this, gold went into a long-term bear phase, reaching a bottom of $250 per ounce in 1999. Then things changed yet again and gold went into a bull phase. By 2010, the commodity soared to $1,400 an ounce. It was actually one of the top investments during the decade.

It seems that investors still look at gold as a substitute for the paper currency, especially the U.S. dollar. And there are major concerns that the dollar will experience a long-term decline because of the massive budget deficits. In other words, investors think that the U.S. government will essentially pay for these deficits by "printing money," which is likely to lead to inflation.

ALUMINUM AND COPPER

Aluminum is the second most frequently used metal in the world, with copper coming in third. The most commonly used metal is steel. For the past 25 years, copper production has gone from 8 million tons to over 15 million tons. As for aluminum, it has gone from 15 million tons to 32 million tons during the same period.

Aluminum and copper are essential for industrial growth, as well as technology products. Much of the production of copper is from Chile and the United States. The bigger producers of aluminum are China, Russia, and Canada. The growth in emerging economies is likely to continue to be a driver of demand for aluminum and copper. Yet these commodities are highly sensitive to the economy. For example, during the 2008–2009 global recession, there was a sharp drop in the prices of these commodities. The result was also steep declines in the stock prices of companies like Alcoa.

COMMODITY INDEXES

Besides shorting an individual commodity, it is also possible to do the same with a basket of commodities. This is done by shorting a commodity index.

Examples of popular commodity indexes include the Dow Jones–AIG Commodity Index, the Deutsche Bank Liquid Commodity Index, the Goldman Sachs Commodity Index, the Reuters/Jefferies Commodity Research Bureau Index, and the Rogers International Commodities Index. There are also a variety of exchange-traded funds (ETFs) to select from to short. Or, an investor can short a future against a commodity index.

All commodity indexes share the same characteristics. A commodity index must track only commodities that are traded on an exchange. If not, it would be extremely difficult to get accurate prices. What's more, a commodity index can only be for those commodities that can be delivered. This means financial instruments are excluded.

But commodity indexes will certainly have differences. Take the Deutsche Bank Liquid Commodity Index. This index has a 55-percent weighting in energy fuels. The reason is that a large proportion of the world's trading is in this sector. Another reason for the high concentration in this sector is that the Deutsche Bank index tries to avoid "rebalancing." This is the process of selling off commodities as they become a larger part of the index. While this helps to improve diversification, it can be costly as well as reduce overall returns. But some indexes, like the Dow Jones–AIG Commodity Index, will actually have strict monthly rebalancing.

TRADING COMMODITIES

There are several ways to short commodities. First of all, an investor can focus on "commodity producers." These are companies that explore and mine for commodities. For example, if gold is expected to fall, you can take a short position in a variety of gold companies.

While this is straightforward, there may be a problem. A commodity producer may have "hedged its positions." This means it has purchased futures or options that essentially short the commodity. The result is there is downside protection. A decline in commodities will probably not result in a significant drop in revenues and profits. Plus, management may also find ways to counter the situation, such as with share buybacks or even the sale of the company.

Another approach is to short the stock market of a country, which is dependent on a commodity. A case would be Russia, which relies heavily on oil. Its economy will often swoon when the price of this commodity falls. But yet again, there may still be offsetting factors. The economy may find growth elsewhere or it might even try to hedge its position. Thus, when shorting commodities, investors will often use an alternative approach. These include futures and ETFs.

FUTURES

The origins of the futures markets go back to the mid-1850s, when the United States started to become a national power. It was getting too inefficient for farmers to transport their harvest to distribution locations and enter into contracts. There were many problems, including bad weather and not enough storage. It was often the case that commodities would rot. To make the process better, a group of merchants banded together in 1848 to create the Chicago Board of Trade (CBOT). It was the first commodities exchange.

At first, the CBOT used "forward contracts." This allowed a farmer to sell his or her crop at a future date. While it was a big help, there was still a problem. Every contract had to be negotiated, which was costly and time-consuming. So by 1865, the CBOT introduced "futures contracts." With these, there were standard contract terms. In fact, these are the same as they are today. A futures contract will have the following terms:

- **Description:** This is the name of the commodity, such as corn, wheat, and so on.
- **Quantity:** This is the amount, which depends on the commodity. For example, one corn contract will be for 5,000 bushels and one oil contract will be for 10,000 barrels.
- **Delivery Data:** This is the time that the buyer of a futures contract will receive the quantity specified under the futures contract. Again, the dates depend on the commodity —but they are usually on a quarterly basis.

Actually, a futures contract is similar to an options contract. There is a buyer and a seller for each contract at a fixed price and amount. But the main difference is that on the expiration of a futures contract, the parties must meet their contractual obligations. If a futures contract is a "tangible" commodity, then this means there will be a physical settlement. So if you buy a futures contract on pork bellies, you will get delivery of this asset when the contract expires. Or, if the contract is "intangible"—like a stock index or interest rates—then there will be a cash settlement. However, in most cases, the trader will buy an offsetting futures contract to eliminate having to take these delivery options.

You can trade futures on various exchanges, which include the Chicago Mercantile Exchange and the Intercontinental Exchange. There are also many foreign exchanges like the Dubai Mercantile Exchange, the Korea Exchange, the Singapore Exchange, the Tokyo Commodity Exchange, and so on. A critical service of these futures exchanges is their "clearing houses." Basically, this means that the exchange will be on the other side of each trade. Thus, if a party fails to deliver the commodity or settle the necessary cash requirement, there will not be a default. No doubt, this helps create confidence in the exchange since there is no counterparty risk.

One of the interesting aspects of futures is that for everyone who takes a long position, there needs to be someone who takes a short position. In other words, both parties in the transaction are betting on the commodity going in opposite directions. Needless to say, short selling will never be banned from the futures markets.

TRADING FUTURES

To engage in futures, you will need to set up an account with a brokerage firm. The company must be a registered member of the "Commodities Futures Trading Commission (CFTC)," which is the federal agency that regulates the futures markets. You will also need to set up a margin account. But it is not like the one you would establish for short selling stock. Instead, a "futures margin account" will essentially track your position in each futures contract on a daily basis. If your margin percentage falls below the minimum level, the broker will request more cash or the position will be immediately closed out.

There's also another key difference between a short-selling and futures margin account. With a stock, you may have no less than 50 percent of the position in your account. But with a futures contract, the cash is often much lower. It could be only 5 percent to 10 percent of the futures contract value.

In addition, the futures markets have their own restrictions. An important one is a "market limit." For example, corn is allowed to move up 20 cents per contract—up or down—in a day. This is to help bring order to the market. Yet this can also cause problems. Let's say corn is trading at $2 per contract and it falls to $1.60. It will actually not start trading again until two days. Thus, a market limit can be quite disruptive for a futures trader.

One important thing to keep in mind when using a futures margin account is that, given the volatility and margin rules, the account can be wiped out quickly. As a result, an investor needs to understand his or her amount of leverage and the risks involved in the portfolio.

ANALYSIS

When it comes to shorting commodities, investors have a variety of options. One approach is to use technical analysis, which is often for short-term moves. Some of the main charts to focus on—those that show bearishness—include the Double Top and the Head and Shoulders.

Another way to find short opportunities is to analyze supply-and-demand trends. Obviously, investors want to see a weak demand and an excess supply. This will drive down prices for commodities. But it takes lots of research, such as by using resources from trade associations for the commodity. Another helpful resource is the Commodity Research Bureau's CRB Yearbook. Many investors consider it a bible for commodities trading.

When doing research, a short seller will look at some key factors. First, there is "the supply side." Simply put, you want to get a rough number on the total amount of the commodity on the global market. Next, you will research "the growth trends." Will new mines become operable? When? How much supply will they produce? Then there is "the demand side." What are the current consumption levels of the commodity on the world markets? And how is the world economy performing? If it is trending downwards, then expect a lessening of demand for the commodity.

It also is important to factor in other "counter trends." For example, is the commodity a big part of an industry that is ailing? Or is the commodity suffering from a disruption in technology? This was the case when there was less demand for copper as telecommunications companies moved from land-line phones to mobile phones. Finally, the last key element in the pricing of commodities is "carrying charges." This represents the storage, insurance, spoilage, and so on. For large amounts of commodities, these costs are not insignificant. Because of this, the futures contract prices will usually be higher for those that have later delivery dates. This is called the "contango."

Short sellers must remember that supply-demand dynamics may not necessarily be foolproof. Consider that during the late 1970s, the price of oil continued to increase despite a global recession and oversupply in the markets. Why? One reason is that there was a speculative bubble in the markets. There was also uncertainty about the geopolitical situation. In fact, Iran and Iraq would eventually go to war, which was disruptive to the oil markets.

THE COT INDEX

Some investors will look at overall trends in the actual trading of futures to get a sense of the market direction. For example, they may focus on the activities of "commercial traders." These are commodity producers that buy futures to hedge their positions in the market. Of course, these organizations have top-notch analysts and resources to gauge the direction of the market.

For the most part, commodity producers will be fairly steady in their positions. However, a short seller will certainly be alerted if there is a sudden change. One way to detect this is to use the "COT Index," which trader Stephen Briese created in the early 1990s. It compares the net long and short positions of commercial traders. The closer the COT Index is to zero, the more bearish is the futures market. The index actually hit zero in October 2007, which was at the onset of the recession and a plunge in commodities prices.

20-YEAR CYCLES

Over the past 100 years, the commodities markets have seen consistent cycles. The main bull markets tend to last 18 to 20 years.

Examples include 1906 to 1923, 1933 to 1953, and 1968 to 1982. Also, it appears that the latest bull market began in the late 1990s and has continued through 2010. When the commodities markets are in the bull phase, the prices can surge to incredible heights. Consider that from 1966 to 1974, sugar went from 1.4 cents to 66 cents. And of course, the bear markets can be brutal—and last for several decades. After all, oil plunged from $40 to $10 a barrel from 1980 to 1985.

While some may consider these commodities cycles a fluke, there is actually a rationale to them. First of all, commodities are essential for society. We need oil, grains, livestock, and so on. If anything, these will likely see stronger growth in the upcoming decades because of the major changes in China, India, and other emerging economies. There are even signs that Africa will see a renaissance. Yet it is expensive and time-consuming to find, extract, and transport commodities. Just look at oil. As it gets tougher to find new sources, oil producers must engage in deepwater drilling or exploration in remote areas of the world (such as Nigeria). It can easily cost billions of dollars and take a decade to get a well that is producing sufficient oil, and the result of this is that the commodities industry goes through long periods of underinvestment and overinvestment. When prices are higher, producers will get aggressive in finding new supplies. Once these come online, there will be lower prices. These can persist for a long time since it can take a decade to exhaust the excess commodities on the market.

The irony is that the bull/bear markets in commodities are opposite of the bull/bear markets in equities. Again, there is logic to this. When commodities prices are lower, companies will have lower costs, which will boost profits. This should mean stronger stock prices. So how do commodities react to recessions? Commodities have shown to be resistant to downturns. Keep in mind that one of the strongest commodities bull markets was during the 1930s.

PROFESSIONAL INVESTORS

Because of the complexities of futures trading—and keeping track of the day-to-day moves of commodities—many investors will use professional money managers. One option is mutual funds, which typically have low minimum investment levels and are easy to set up. But as with any type of mutual fund, it is important to look at the fees (which can be relatively higher for commodities funds) as well as the track record. Finally, there are not many commodities mutual funds on the market—and they may not necessarily short the market either. And even for those that do, the performance has been uneven. True, the typical fund scored a nice 14.1-percent return in 2008. But for the most part, these types of funds are relatively new and it will take more time to see if they are viable alternatives.

Another approach is to use a "managed futures account." This is a pool of investment funds from investors. They will each set up a typical futures account but have one or more professional managers trade it. This is done by giving the managers discretion on the account. The managers are known as "commodity trading advisors," or CTAs. They are registered by the Commodity Futures Trading Commission and must pass an exam, as well as a background check.

Of course, it is important to do extensive research on the managers. Have there been any regulatory infractions? What is their track record—in good and bad times? What is their approach on shorting commodities? While a CTA will not provide much detail on their strategies—which they often consider to be proprietary—they should provide broad ideas about their investment principles. They should also discuss their areas of expertise, such as oil, metals, and so on. At the same time, you need to periodically monitor the activity in the managed futures account. Are things getting worse? How are they performing against the relevant indexes?

The fee structure for a managed futures account is similar to a hedge fund's fee structure. The fund will typically get 2 percent of all assets under management and 20 percent of the profits. What's more, the minimum investment may be steep. In some cases, it may be $1 million or more. But over the years, Wall Street firms have developed more products with more affordable investment minimums.

Investing in commodities is certainly a specialized area. You will not only need to understand the dynamics of particular commodities but also have a good grasp of futures trading. The good news is that there are a variety of online futures trading firms that are focused on individual investors, like FXCM.com.

In the next chapter, we will take a look at how to short markets with funds. For many investors, this will be the most common method for short selling.

CHAPTER 14

Shorting with Mutual Funds, Hedge Funds, ETFs, and Inverted ETFs

Key Concepts

- Using funds as an alternative to short selling
- Looking at the advantages and disadvantages of mutual funds, ETFs, and hedge funds

The traditional short-sale trade is borrowing shares and selling them on the open market. The hope is to buy them back at a cheaper price in the future. As seen in Chapter 10, there are risks and costs to this approach, such as margin interest, short squeezes, and buy-ins. But a short seller has other options. These include futures and options. However, these also have their drawbacks. Because of the high leverage, an option or future can easily go to zero.

In light of all this, many investors prefer to use professional money managers and simpler products. The most common include mutual funds, hedge funds, and exchange-traded funds.

MUTUAL FUNDS

A "mutual fund" is a pool of investor money, which focuses on a certain investment strategy like blue chips, growth companies, and even short-selling products. Since the early 1980s, mutual funds have become extremely popular, especially for 401(k) portfolios. Although, in light of the fees and tough market conditions from 2000 to 2010, the category has seen a slowdown. In fact, a new type of fund—called the exchange-traded fund (EFT)—has become increasingly popular for individual investors. Yet the fact remains that mutual funds offer investors a cost-effective way to build a portfolio. But before looking at the advantages—as well as the disadvantages—let's first get a basic understanding of how mutual funds work.

An investment company—like Fidelity or Schwab—will sponsor the creation of a mutual fund. In essence, the fund will be its own company, with a board of directors and portfolio managers. A key part of the fund is its "Net Asset Value (NAV)." The NAV is equal to the sum of all the fund's assets minus the liabilities and expenses. The result is then divided by the number of shares outstanding. By regulation, a mutual fund is required to report the NAV at the close of each trading day. Of course, the goal of all mutual funds is to consistently increase the NAV over time. If not, there are likely to be dissatisfied investors, who might wind up redeeming their shares. There are two main types of mutual funds—open-end funds and closed-end funds.

Open-end Mutual Funds

The "open-end mutual fund" is, by far, the most common mutual fund. Such a fund will issue new shares when investors buy more and reduce the number of shares when there are redemptions. The result is that the value of the shares will always *equal* the Net Asset Value. A big problem for open-end mutual funds is when there is a sudden spike in redemptions. Under this situation, the fund may not have enough cash on hand to meet these claims. As a result, there will be a need to sell the securities in the portfolios. Since this often occurs in a down market, the losses can be substantial. Then again, a short seller may see these redemptions as a sign that an industry or investment category is experiencing weakness. Thus, there may be an opportunity to short this area of the market.

Closed-end Mutual Funds

Next, there is the "closed-end mutual fund." This is when an investment company creates a fund and sells shares in a public offering. You will find many closed-end funds traded on the

American Stock Exchange. And yes, you will need to pay a commission when you buy and sell shares in this type of investment.

Unlike an open-end mutual fund, the number of shares stays constant and the investment managers have a fixed amount of capital to invest. This often means that the stock price is at a *discount* to the Net Asset Value. Why? There are a variety of reasons. One is that the management expenses can be higher as a percentage of the assets. This is because closed-end mutual funds tend to have smaller asset bases. Moreover, such funds do not have as much trading volume, which can result in lower valuations. But some closed-end funds are quite popular, which is certainly the case with Warren Buffett's Berkshire Hathaway. Because of his legendary investment acumen, the stock actually trades at a premium to its NAV.

Another common type of closed-end mutual fund is the "real estate investment trust (REIT)." As the name implies, this is a fund that invests in real estate assets like commercial properties, apartments, homes, and even mortgages. But short sellers tend to avoid REITs. A key reason is that they usually pay relatively high rates of dividends. This is because real estate is primarily an income-driven investment. So with high dividends, this can make it expensive for short sellers (who are required to pay them to the party they borrowed the shares from).

Despite all this, REITs may still be an option for short sellers. For example, one scenario is if it appears that the company will have to reduce or even eliminate its dividends. Actually, this was common for mortgage REITs during the financial meltdown of 2008. To spot a dividend problem, a short seller will look at a variety of factors. One is if a REIT has a heavy debt load. In such a case, it becomes more difficult to pay the dividend. Next, a short seller will find the main locations of the real estate. If these areas are fairly depressed, this will be a drag on income.

ADVANTAGES AND DISADVANTAGES OF MUTUAL FUNDS FOR SHORT SELLING

Advantages

Mutual funds are quite versatile and have seen lots of innovation over the years. Keep in mind that there are thousands of mutual funds on the market that cater to a wide variety of investment strategies and asset classes. And mutual funds certainly have many advantages. For example, the minimum investment levels are affordable.[1] They may be as low as $100 (although the typical amount is $1,000). Additionally, many have automatic investment programs. This means that you can invest a fixed amount in a fund every month or quarter. It is an effective way to build a position.

Another key benefit of mutual funds is professional management. You will get full-time experts who analyze investment opportunities and construct a portfolio to meet the fund's objectives. Mutual funds also provide investors with a certain amount of protection. This is certainly comforting in light of recent scandals in the financial industry, such as those involving Bernie Madoff and Robert Allen. By SEC regulation, the assets of a fund are kept separate from the fund company, so it is extremely difficult for the portfolio managers to abscond with the money. What's more, the SEC has extensive regulations for the mutual fund industry, which means you have access to lots of disclosures. A key document is the "prospectus," which has a fund's strategy, management bios, fee structure, holdings, historical returns, and so on. While the disclosure statements are getting easier to understand—because of recent reforms—they are still legalistic and complicated. But there are a variety of third-party resources, such as Morningstar, that help out. Also, another good option is to visit the mutual fund's Web site. You should find helpful resources there.

Disadvantages

Like with any type of investment structure, however, mutual funds do have their drawbacks. Perhaps the most important is "performance." Unfortunately, a large number of mutual funds underperform their market benchmarks. True, one reason is the fee structure. But the fact remains that it is extremely difficult for portfolio managers to maintain consistent returns—especially with regards to short selling. One reason for this is that the mutual fund industry has a tough time attracting top-notch operators in the business. Why?

---

[1] There are cases in which a mutual fund may have a hefty minimum investment, say, $10,000 or even $25,000, but these instances are rather rare and occur when mutual funds want more sophisticated investors who can stomach the volatility.

They will opt to go to a hedge fund, where the fees are much more lucrative and there is often more flexibility in terms of investment strategies. True, there are certainly a variety of short-oriented mutual funds that have strong managers and track records. But of course, it is important to take the time to research their performance.

Speaking of short-oriented mutual funds, consistent returns seem to be a problem within this recent category of investments. The reason is that until 1998, there were strict regulations on allowing short trades. However, this has been loosened up and mutual funds have much more flexibility. It also can be difficult for short-oriented funds to get the attention of investors. So it is not uncommon for these types of funds to eventually close down. For these reasons, it is important to study a short-oriented fund's overall performance. How has it done in bear markets? Has it shown strong returns during these times? Has the fund been able to minimize losses during bull markets?

Evaluating the Performance of a Mutual Fund

One way to get a sense of the performance is to look at the "r-squared coefficient," which you can find from a third party like Morningstar. This is a statistic that measures the volatility of a mutual fund compared to an index. If r-squared is 1, then there is a 100-percent correlation. On the other hand, an r-squared of 0 means there is absolutely no correlation. For the most part, investors try to look for non-correlated investments to add to a portfolio. This helps to reduce the overall risk and improve the diversification. And, if a short-oriented fund is effectively managed, it should have a relatively low r-squared.

An investor also needs to be mindful of a mutual fund's expenses. Running such an operation is not cheap and involves costs for offices, software, commissions, and salaries for top-notch money managers. The "expense ratio" shows these costs as a percentage of the Net Asset Value. A typical long-only fund may have an expense ratio of 1 percent to 1.5 percent. However, a short-oriented fund may have one in excess of 2 percent. While this may not sound like a lot, it can take a toll on returns over time.

Why are higher fees charged? One reason is that short-oriented funds often have lower asset sizes. This means there is not as much room to spread out the costs. Next, a short-oriented fund will probably have high borrowing costs for the short positions.

Then, there is high "turnover." This is the amount of the portfolio that is sold during a year. For instance, a turnover ratio of 100 percent would mean that the portfolio has been completely sold—on average. In the case of short selling, the turnover tends to be high—say even more than 200 percent. Basically, short selling is usually not for long-term positions. Instead, an effective short seller will often be a good trader. But high turnover means higher commission costs, which boosts the expense ratio.

There will also be something else: taxes. With large amounts of short-term capital gains distributions, the tax load can be relatively higher than long-only funds. For this reason, it may make sense to have a short-oriented fund in a tax shelter, like an IRA.

Besides expenses, a mutual fund may also have a "load," which is a commission to buy or sell the fund. While many funds are no-load, this may not necessarily be the case with short-oriented funds. And yes, a load can easily eat into returns. Keep in mind that mutual funds will quote a load percentage that actually understates the charge. For example, suppose you want to buy the Short XYZ Fund, which has an NAV of $10 and a load of 5 percent. To calculate the real commission level, you will do the following:

First you will calculate the offer price:

$$\text{Offer Price} = \text{NAV} / (1 - \text{Load Percentage})$$
$$= \$10 / (1.0 - 0.05)$$
$$= \$10.53$$

Next, you will calculate the effective load rate:

$$\text{Effective Load Rate} = \text{Load Charge} / \text{NAV}$$
$$= \$0.53 / \$10$$
$$= 5.3\%$$

Besides this, there are other types of loads to factor when thinking of purchasing a short-oriented investment. In fact, some funds even charge loads on the reinvestment of dividends. If so, try to get this waived. There may also be a "back-end load." This is a load charged when you redeem shares in a fund. Generally, the percentage is lower than a front-loaded fund. But this can be misleading. How? The reason is that by the time you redeem shares, they may be at a higher level. As a result, the total dollar amount of the commission may wind up being higher. Or, a fund may have a "12(b)-1 fee." This is also known as a "distribution fee." But regardless of the label, it is essentially a load. A mutual fund may charge a 12(b)-1 fee on an annual basis, with a maximum of 1 percent.

But, some mutual funds will actually provide discounts, especially for investors who make large commitments. This is usually if the investment is $100,000 to $200,000. If so, the fund will reduce the load or even eliminate it. So in light of the burden of loads, why do investors pay them? First of all, you may do so because you think the portfolio manager is top-notch and you are willing to pay a premium. Or, you have a financial advisor that is paid based on the types of investments selected.

TYPES OF SHORT-ORIENTED FUNDS

Even though there are a relatively small amount of short-oriented funds, you will still be able to find one that fits a main category. A common one is the "market-neutral fund." This is where the portfolio manager will invest an equal amount in long and short positions to factor out the overall movements in the market. This strategy usually performs better in down markets—but tends to be limited during bull markets. There are also "long-short funds," which are actually similar to market-neutral funds. However, with long-short funds, a portfolio manager will have the leeway to take a short or long bias in the portfolio. In other words, he or she will be able to engage in market timing, which can be a tough thing to get right (at least over the long haul). And yet another type of short-oriented fund is the so-called "bear fund." As the name implies, this is where the main focus is on short positions. There are only a handful of bear funds on the market.

The mutual fund industry also has been making some innovations in short-oriented funds. Perhaps one of the most interesting is a "130/30 fund." Essentially, this is a mutual fund that has 130 percent of its assets in long positions and 30 percent in short positions. This is a recent phenomenon, with the first funds coming on the market in 2004. But why use 130/30? Part of the reason is the 1940

Act, which imposed portfolio restrictions on mutual funds. Also, a 130/30 fund is considered to be fairly optimal for diversification.

Yet the fact remains that there is still material risk since a 130/30 fund needs to borrow money. While this can certainly magnify returns if the portfolio manager makes good decisions, the opposite is possible as well. And the losses can be significant—at least compared to a non-leveraged mutual fund. Another problem for 130/30 funds is tax inefficiency. Because of heavy trading activity, an investor may wind up with a large short-term capital gain. As a result, it may make more sense to have a 130/30 fund in a tax-advantaged account like an individual retirement account (IRA).

HEDGE FUNDS

The origins of hedge funds go back to the 1950s. Interestingly enough, it was a sociologist—Alfred Winslow Jones—who came up with the concept. He believed that stock-picking strategies and mutual funds were woefully inadequate in getting strong returns. He wanted to create a portfolio that would not only buy shares but also short them. Over time, this would reduce overall risks. Yes, Jones wanted to find a way to hedge a portfolio.

To this end, he structured the investment as a private partnership. Next, there would be an incentive structure that would encourage strong returns. A money manager would get 1 percent to 2 percent of the money in the fund and also get 20 percent of the profits, which is called the "carried interest." And Jones certainly proved himself to be a hedge fund visionary. From 1949 to 1966, his hedge fund saw returns of 27 percent per year. This compared to an average return of 11 percent annually for the Dow. No doubt, this attracted the attention of the investment world. And by the 1970s, the modern hedge fund industry started to emerge.

Advantages of Hedge Funds

As with any investment structure, hedge funds have their advantages and disadvantages. One of the most important positive factors is that the industry attracts some of the world's top investors. Of course, this is mainly due to the high compensation structure. Consider that some hedge fund managers, like Steven Cohen and

Jim Simons, have produced annual returns of 30 percent plus per year over more than a decade. What's more, hedge funds allow for a tremendous amount of flexibility. A portfolio manager can short a security or even use advanced derivatives like options and futures.

Yet another advantage is that there are several fee protection mechanisms. One is "the high water mark." The purpose of this is to prohibit a fund from charging the carried interest after there has been a drop in value. For example, suppose the fund has a value of $100 million. Then, within a few months, it drops to $80 million. There can be no carried interest until the fund gets back to $100 million, which is the high water mark. However, there is one problem with high water marks. If a fund has a big drop, then the portfolio managers may decide to close down the operation because it would take too long to overcome the high water mark.

Next, a second fee protection mechanism within hedge funds is "the hurdle rate." With this, a hedge fund must exceed a benchmark by a certain level before getting the performance fee. This may mean that it must be 0.5 percent or 1 percent higher than the S&P 500 for the month. However, hurdle rates are not common.

Disadvantages of Hedge Funds

So what are the problems with hedge funds? The minimums can be high, such as $1 million or more. In fact, some hedge funds do not even allow new investors (especially those funds with strong track records).

Even if you can afford the minimums, there may be other problems with hedge funds. For example, because hedge funds are mostly for wealthy and sophisticated investors, the regulations are not as stringent as compared to alternatives like mutual funds. This lack of regulation can certainly be a problem, as hedge funds have attracted a variety of fraudulent players.

Size can also present itself as an issue. Over the years, some hedge funds have attracted huge amounts of capital. For a hedge fund manager, it is hard to say "no" to these inflows. After all, a 2-percent management fee can turn into a substantial amount of money when a fund has multibillions. Yet a large fund could ultimately be detrimental to investors. A portfolio manager may have to expand into new categories and take higher risks.

There are also problems with diversification in hedge funds. To invest in several funds is likely to be out of reach for many investors. So to deal with this, one option is to use a "hedge fund of funds." This is a money manager that takes a smaller amount of investment from many investors and pools the cash. Thus, it is easier to place the money across various funds. However, even a hedge fund of funds has its drawbacks. First, it charges a fee on top of the fees from the underlying hedge funds. This can certainly eat into returns. Next, a hedge fund of funds manager has lots of influence. How do you know if the decisions will ultimately make sense? In other words, it is important to do a background check on the manager.

Even with such help, there are risks. One is secrecy. Because a hedge fund is a private partnership, there are few requirements for disclosure. An investor may have little idea about the holdings and investment strategies—since these are often considered to be proprietary. There may also be "lock-ups." This means that the investors are prevented from redeeming their positions for a fixed period of time, such as a year. While this is usually to the benefit of investors— since it reduces the adverse impact of lots of selling in a short period of time—there are exceptions. This was definitely the case during 2008, when the markets plunged and investors were unable to get ready access to their funds.

EXCHANGE-TRADED FUNDS (EFTS)

Like a mutual fund, an "exchange-traded fund (ETF)" is a pool of investors' assets that are invested in stocks and bonds. But an ETF usually does not have active management from a portfolio manager. Instead, the portfolio is based on some type of index like the S&P 500. Because of this approach, the management costs of an ETF are relatively low compared to actively managed mutual funds. For example, the typical expense ratio for a stock-based ETF is 0.40 percent or so. Even funds that focus on international markets are at a low 0.50 percent.

An ETF is also listed on a stock exchange. This means an investor can buy, sell, or short the security when the market is open (the commissions are equivalent to a typical stock). This means it is possible to engage in day trading with ETFs. ETFs also allow for risk-management strategies like stop-loss and limit orders, and they make it unlikely that you will receive few capital gains distribution. This is based on the structure of the fund. In other words, ETFs are highly tax-efficient.

For a short seller, an ETF is certainly useful. A key reason is that this type of security allows the investor to take advantage of a myriad of themes. You can short an ETF that focuses on industry sectors like biotech, utilities, and even solar. ETFs are also effective in targeting foreign markets. In fact, top short sellers like Jim Chanos have been expanding into this area. Consider that one of his biggest themes is China. According to his analysis, he thinks the country is in the midst of a massive real estate bubble, driven by too much debt. When it pops, he thinks the stock markets will plunge. He even goes so far as to say that the Chinese government is cooking the books and the growth rates are not as high as reported.

Yet Chanos has had difficulties finding effective ways to short China. True, he can use a China-based ETF. But for an investor with substantial funds (he manages $6 billion), he has had to look at other places to make the trade. One is to look at those industries that will be negatively impacted by a crash in China. These would be coal, construction, and other infrastructure companies. And yes, it is possible to find ETFs in these categories as well.

Another popular short opportunity in global markets was the European debt crisis of 2010. There were concerns that countries like Portugal, Spain, and Greece would actually default on their government loans. As a result, interest rates on their debt skyrocketed and the European Union (EU) had to launch an aggressive plan to avoid major problems. To capitalize on the situation, investors aggressively shorted ETFs.

INVERSE EXCHANGE-TRADED FUNDS

In 2006, Wall Street introduced "inverted exchange-traded funds (ETFs)." This means that if the index goes up 1 percent, the ETF will fall 1 percent. In other words, an inverted ETF is short the index. This is done by using highly sophisticated strategies that involve options and futures. Because of this, there is technically not a pure 1–to–1 relationship—but it is usually close.

But Wall Street did not stop there. Since then, there have been the introduction of inverted ETFs that are leveraged. For example, a 2X inverted ETF would increase 2 percent for every 1-percent drop in the index. And yes, there are even ETFs that have 3X leverage. While 1X inverted ETFs are quite effective in playing investment themes, the leveraged versions are quite volatile. Thus, they should be used with much caution.

NAKED SHORT SELLING

What if you short a stock but do so without borrowing the shares? This would mean that you are engaged in "naked short selling." It is also referred to as a "fail to deliver" trade. An investor may do this because of difficulties in finding shares to borrow. Or the cost of a short sale may be prohibitive. However, in the United States—as well as many other foreign stock exchanges—naked short selling is illegal. This is according to SEC Regulation SHO of the Securities and Exchange Commission.

Why is this so? The belief is that naked short selling could potentially allow for an unlimited position, which could ultimately drive down the stock. Actually, this was one of the complaints during the financial meltdown of 2008. Despite this, there is still much controversy. That is, various companies and traders believe that naked short selling is fairly common but the laws are rarely enforced. In fact, a sudden rise in failed-to-deliver trades may indicate that a stock is experiencing heavy levels of naked short selling. For example, Regulation SHO provides for a "Threshold Security List," which shows a stock where more than 0.5 percent of the outstanding shares have failed to deliver for five business days. Ironically enough, short sellers consider this a guide for companies that may be good short trades.

When it comes to using funds, the most common approach for individual investors is mutual funds. Good choices would include market-neutral and long-short funds. But of course, an investor needs to do research, especially on the performance and backgrounds of the portfolio managers.

In the next chapter, we will look at special situation shorts. These involve categories like IPOs, tech companies, and even foreign currencies.

CHAPTER 15

Special
Situation Shorts

Key Concepts

- Discussing special categories of the market, like tech stocks and IPOs, that have short-selling opportunities
- Showing how to short foreign currencies

There are certain types of stocks that are often favorites for short sellers. They include IPOs, spin-offs, finance companies, and technology companies. These types of companies often have special types of dynamics, especially in terms of risk. So if a short seller has a good handle on the industry, the returns can be particularly strong. There is also another area of the markets that has become quite popular for short sellers: foreign exchange. This is especially the case as investors look for returns overseas. But as with any specialized area of investing, there are complexities and unique trading strategies involved with each of these shorting opportunities.

SHORTING IPOs

An "initial public offering (IPO)" is the first time a company issues stock to the public. The company usually needs enough critical mass to get the interest of shareholders. Some of the requirements are as follows:

Requirements of IPOs

- Revenues of over $100 million
- Profitable or approaching profitability
- A strong management team
- A defensible business
- A strong growth rate, such as with revenues increasing at double digits

As you can see, the above indicates a typical growth company. And of course, some IPOs have turned into mega-companies within a short period of time, such as Microsoft, Starbucks, and eBay.

How the IPO Process Works

Let's take an example to see how the IPO process works. Suppose XYZ Corp. meets the requirements for going public and wants to raise more capital. The company will meet with various "underwriters," which are Wall Street firms. Examples include Goldman Sachs, BofA Merrill Lynch, and Morgan Stanley. These firms will make presentations to XYZ Corp. to get the engagement. If they win, they will then conduct due diligence on the company. The underwriter wants to make sure that the financials meet GAAP requirements and that the business plan is strong enough to attract investors.

XYZ Corp. and the underwriter will then draft the "prospectus." This is a long document—which can easily be several hundred pages—that has the necessary disclosures for investors, such as the financials, the business plan, key contracts, executive compensation, and so on. XYZ Corp. will then file this with the Securities and Exchange Commission (SEC). Over several months, the SEC will make comments on the S-1 filing and the company will make changes. When there are no issues left, the SEC will declare the offering "effective." This means that XYZ Corp. can sell the shares to the public.

Before doing this, the company and the underwriter will have "a road show." This involves many presentations to investors across the country—and perhaps certain countries (you can find these at www.retailroadshow.com). Investors will ask questions and then put in indications of interest. The underwriter will get a sense of the demand for the offering and establish a price range. For a typical IPO, the amount raised will be between $100 million to $200 million. But interestingly enough, the underwriter will often underprice the IPO. Why? This will create a spike in the price on the first day of trading, which can easily be 20 percent to 30 percent. This underpricing encourages investors to participate. It also gets some public relations for the firm.

Keep in mind, however, that this strategy can sometimes backfire and lead to extreme overvaluation. This was certainly the case during the dot-com boom. For example, in December 1999, the IPO of VA Linux increased nearly 700 percent on its first day of trading. This was the case even though the company was losing money. Within a few years, the shares were below a dollar. While this is an extreme example, it does illustrate an important characteristic of IPOs: many eventually fizzle out. The competition gets more intense or the market potential is not as big as expected. Or, there could be missteps like product delays.

There are some technical barriers to shorting IPOs that short sellers should be mindful of. In fact, it can be nearly impossible to short them during the first month of trading. The reason is that it takes time for brokerages to get enough borrowable shares. But this is usually not a problem as there should still be opportunities for short sellers.

Another key factor to look at is the stature of the underwriters, which is often a predictor of the success or failure of an IPO. If a top-tier underwriter is involved, this helps to minimize the risks. Short sellers will definitely be interested if an underwriter has little experience or is not well-known. They will often look at the overall track record.

Best-Efforts IPOs and Direct IPOs

A short seller will be alerted if a company has a "best-efforts IPO." The general approach is for a "firm commitment offering." This is where the underwriter will guarantee the proceeds from the IPO. However, with a best-efforts approach, the underwriter will guarantee nothing. It's a sign that the underwriter sees risks with the company.

Another problematic offering is a "direct IPO." This is when a company does not even use an underwriter; instead, it will handle the process on its own. This poses lots of risks for investors since there is no underwriter to pursue due diligence. There is also little aftermarket support, such as analyst coverage. The result is the performance of the stock is usually fairly weak.

Evaluating IPOs

When evaluating an IPO, short sellers will also spend lots of time analyzing the prospectus. While it is often complicated, there are certain areas to spot dangers. One area worth looking at is the "Management" section. Here you will see the bios of the senior executives and board members. Short sellers will consider the following: Do they have strong industry experience? How much background do they have with public companies? It is not uncommon for newly public companies to have inexperienced executives, who may ultimately make bad decisions.

Another helpful section is "Competition." It will show the main rivals for the company—even indirect ones. Does the company really have a differentiated product or service that sets it apart from the competition? If not, then the company is likely to be in a tough sales environment. This was the case with Vonage, a provider of Internet-based phone services. While the company had a good brand and a cost-effective service, it was not enough to deal with the competition. First, major telecom companies could undercut the company, such as by offering a bundle of services, including cable and wireless Internet. Next, there was a patent suit from Verizon. Within a couple of years, Vonage had to negotiate an expensive settlement. In other words, it is also a good idea for short sellers to read the "Litigation" section of the prospectus.

A short seller will also look at the "lock-up expiration," which is a contract provision found in most IPOs. It essentially prohibits company employees and key investors from selling shares within the first six months of the offering. The rationale is to prevent undue dumping of the stock. But of course, there may be pent-up demand to do this when the lock-up expires. As a result, a short seller may have an opportunity to trade the stock for a profit.

What's more, short sellers will want to see if there are any "selling shareholders" in the offering. This is when insiders of the company sell a portion or all of their holding at the time of the IPO. If the amounts are 20 percent or more of the offering, then a short seller would be concerned. It shows a lack of confidence in the company.

Another danger sign is "private equity dumping." After all, a private equity firm will have already used a large amount of debt to buy the company. Then they will try ways to cut costs and reduce some of the leverage. After a few years, the private equity firm will try to take the company public. In many cases, the cash from the offering will go to the firm as well to pay down more debt. But the fact remains that there will likely be further pressure on the stock as the private equity firm continues to sell shares over time. Also, there are still risks with the debt. This was definitely the case when the credit markets froze in 2008.

Finally, a short seller will consider "IPO cycles." The market has periodic "windows." This is when the market environment is bullish and offerings tend to do quite well. But underwriters will usually focus on their top-quality companies, in order to get the best results. However, as time goes by, it will get tougher to find these gems and the quality of the IPOs will decline. This should be a good opportunity for short sellers.

SPIN-OFFS AND TRACKING STOCKS

As companies get larger, it often becomes more difficult to manage the operations. A line of business may not have much growth prospects or may require too much capital investments. To deal with such problems, a company may decide to spin off the division. Sometimes this will involve several divisions.

Like an IPO, a spin-off must file a prospectus with the SEC. So it is a good idea to use the same analytical approach as you would with a public offering. But a short seller will need to be careful.

A spin-off may wind up being a good investment for a variety of reasons. One reason is neglect. While part of a larger organization, the division might not have gotten much attention or resources. Next, there are often conflict problems. That is, the parent company might have made it difficult for the division to get new customers. For example, when AT&T owned Lucent—a seller of telecom equipment—some potential companies did not do business with it because it would have benefited a competitor. But by being independent, this was not a problem for Lucent. So after the spin-off, the shares did quite well. What's more, the spin-off company can use its stock to raise additional capital or as currency to buy other companies. The stock can also be used to help motivate employees, such as through stock options and equity rewards.

So what will get the interest of short sellers? There are definitely some red flags:

Red Flags to Watch for in Spin-offs

- **Capital:** The parent company may raise money in the spin-off. But where will this money go? If much of it goes to the parent, then this is definitely a problem for the spin-off company.
- **Debt:** In some cases, the parent company will shift a large amount of debt to the spin-off company. No doubt, this increases the overall risk of the company.
- **Growth:** How has the spin-off company been growing? Is the parent unloading the company because the prospects look dim?

The typical spin-off will include two parts. First, there is a 20-percent equity stake sold to the public. Next, the parent company will distribute the remaining shares over the next few months. What is the reason for this structure? It is so the parent company can make the transaction tax-free. However, the remaining share distribution can dampen the stock price. So this could be an opportunity for a short seller.

But in some cases, a parent company will use a "tracking stock." This means that the parent still has control of the spin-off but will instead create a new stock for the company. This often happens when a major company wants to participate in a major trend. This happened with GE during the dot-com boom. To get a higher stock valuation, the company created a tracking stock for its Internet division, NBCi. It wound up being a dud for investors.

There are also other key problems with tracking stocks. For example, there is no takeover value. After all, the parent company still has control over the asset. Keep in mind that the tracking stock does not have its own board; instead, it is under the power of the parent's board. It is not uncommon that—after the tracking value stock price plunges—the parent will buy it back on the cheap. And there is little shareholders can do, since they only have a minority position.

FINANCE COMPANIES

Short sellers like Jim Chanos have had great success with finance companies. The reason is that the leverage is high. True, this is fine so long as the company makes sound loans and other investments. But of course, this is not always the case. So when there are problems with the asset quality, the finance company's equity can easily be wiped out. This happened to hundreds of banks during 2008, which required the federal Troubled Asset Relief Program (TARP) bailout. Another example was the savings and loan crisis of the late 1980s, which also required a bailout.

Finance companies also have lots of complexity with their financial statements. As a result, many investors will not spend the time necessary to understand the intricacies of the financial statements. So a smart short seller will often find things that the general market overlooks.

Patience is important with shorting finance company stocks. When the economy is strong, the credit will be widely available, even for low-quality institutions. A short seller will likely wait until there are already signs of weakness. This would be especially the case with residential and commercial real estate, which represent a big part of a finance company's assets. But a short seller will dig deeper. For example, a short seller will look for the weakest parts of the real estate market. In 2006 to 2007, these were clearly in California, Arizona, and Florida. A short seller will then look for those finance companies that have exposure in these areas. Next, a short seller will try to determine the quality of the assets. Does the finance company have higher-risk clients? Are they subprime levels? Of course, these showed plunges in valuations as the real estate market cratered.

Another telltale sign is "securitization." This is when a finance company will pool its loans and sell them to Wall Street firms. These securities will then trade on the bond market. But, if a finance company is having trouble securitizing its loans, it is a major red flag. Wall Street is losing confidence in the institution.

TECHNOLOGY SHORTS

Technology companies can be a wild ride—which attracts short sellers. Many wind up getting crushed. Consider Gateway Computers. The company was an early entrant in the personal computer (PC) market and was able to beat out many competitors. Then again, it had a low-cost strategy and savvy marketing. But the company made several missteps, such as getting into the retail business. There were also more and more quality problems with the PCs. Over time, Gateway faded away.

Another prime example is Netscape. The company launched the Internet revolution with its innovative browser and quickly became a tech power. But it was clear that it was attacking Microsoft's operating system dominance, which provoked a fight. Ultimately, Microsoft made its own browser free and available on all versions of Windows. It was a huge blow for Netscape. But the company also made some key strategic mistakes, such as making questionable acquisitions as well as some low-quality product launches.

But perhaps the most interesting story in tech is Apple. Back in the 1990s, this pioneering computer company was slowly losing its way. Losses began to pile up and the company had a confusing product line. At the same time, Microsoft and Intel were getting a large amount of the tech business. But in the late 1990s, Apple's cofounder, Steve Jobs, returned to the company. He made tough changes, such as layoffs and the dumping of various products. The strategy turned out to be a winner as Apple eventually became the most valuable company.

However, tech turnarounds are rare. It is extremely difficult for companies to take on new competitors and remake its product line. It is often too late. So for short sellers, they will try to find tech companies that are in the midst of major transitions. It may take time for the losses to show up and the market shares to crumble, but it is fairly common.

SHORTING FOREIGN CURRENCY

The growth in foreign exchange (FX) trading has soared over the years. Daily transactions have gone from $1.9 trillion in 2004 to

$4 trillion in 2010. In fact, the FX market is the largest in the world.[1] There are many reasons for this. First of all, currencies represent a way to participate in new markets and allow for increased diversification. Next, there has been growing uncertainty about the U.S. dollar. So investors are looking for ways to deal with the risks of a fall in value. What's more, the growth in electronic trading has also spurred trading in FX.

This segment of the market is also attractive to short sellers. For example, they were able to use FX strategies to benefit from the fall of the currencies in troubled nations, such as in Europe in 2010. Despite all this, the U.S. dollar still remains the leader in global currency, representing nearly 85 percent of all transactions.

The FX Market

There are no official exchanges for foreign currency. Instead, it is an "over-the-counter" marketplace. This means that investment banks and other financial institutions facilitate the transactions. Of course, FX trading is more than just about speculators trying to make a profit. It is also the basis of international trade. In fact, many large companies will short foreign currencies to protect their profits from the swings in FX prices.

Central banks are also key participants in the marketplace. They will periodically buy and sell FX in order to pull off monetary policy, such as by moderating inflation. No doubt, changes in the global currency can have a substantial impact on a country's economy. It could result in changes in interest rates, as well as competition from foreign companies.

FX Trading

FX trading is unique. It involves the relative value between one currency against another. This is known as "a pair." For example, it is vague to say that the value of the U.S. dollar has increased. Instead, it must increase compared to another currency, say the Euro. In this case, you can look at a pair called the

---

[1] http://online.wsj.com/article/SB10001424052748704421104575463901 97351049.

USD/EUR. The first currency is called the "base currency" and the second is the "quote" or "counter." Some of the common pairs include the USD/JPY (Japanese yen), USD/GPD (British pound), and USD/CHF (Swiss franc). As for a short seller, he or she can short these pairs. This means that the base currency will fall compared to the quote.

There are many ways to trade currency pairs. They include options and futures. There are also over 40 currency ETFs. A currency pair will trade in "pips," which are the smallest price movements. This is typically 1/100th of 1 percent. Although, some pairs will have their own ratios (such as the Japanese yen). A pip is certainly small. But in the FX market, a small move will often translate into a big change in the market value of the currency pair. The reason is that FX markets use large amounts of leverage. For example, a position may have a 400 to 1 ratio. That is, if the currency value represents $100,000, you will only have to put up $100. Thus, a 1-percent move in the pair would mean an increase of $1,000. Because of this, investors need to be cautious in their trades, as it is not uncommon for traders to lose everything—in a quick period of time. As a result, FX traders will use risk management techniques like stop-loss protections, which are explained in Chapter 10.

An FX trader must also deal with the potential costs of interest. Let's take an example: In Japan, the interest rate is 0.50 percent, but it is 4 percent in the European Union (EU). The 3.50-percent difference is the carrying cost for an investor who is long the euro. But, for the other side of the trade, the investor will be getting the 3.50-percent return. This interest cost means that most traders will focus on short-term positions, say a few days.

It should be no surprise that changes in interest rates have a major impact on the value of currencies. When a country's interest rates are increasing, there will generally be a rise in the value of the currency. The main reason is that global investors will buy the currency in order to benefit from the higher yields. As a result, FX traders will focus carefully on the policies of the major central banks, which can move interest rate levels.

As seen in this chapter, there are a variety of unique niches for short sellers. Often, a short seller will focus on one of them—say finance companies or tech companies. After all, there needs to be lots of industry research to find investment opportunities.

In the next chapter, we will take a look at risk management. Often overlooked, this is extremely important for short sellers because of the potential volatility levels and costs of trading.

CHAPTER 16

Risk Management

Key Concepts

- The different types of risks
- Dealing with risks in a portfolio
- Better risk management with individual trades

Goldman Sachs is one of the largest traders in the world. In 2009, the firm had 131 trading days where it made at least $100 million in net trading profits. This was up from 90 days in 2008. Of course, Goldman Sachs garnered these returns during a tough trading environment. The firm has a highly sophisticated investment platform and a talented group of traders. But another key to Goldman's success is its risk management system. To this end, the firm measures its overall trading risk on a daily basis—called the "value at risk" or VAR. It is the total estimate that Goldman can potentially lose on any given day. Interestingly enough, the most Goldman lost in a single day in 2009 was $153 million.

Risk management is also critical for a successful short seller (keep in mind that Goldman's traders engage frequently in this type of trading). There are two ways to do this: portfolio management and trading rules. But first, it is important to understand the concept of risk.

TYPES OF INVESTMENT RISK

There are many types of risks for investors. To better understand these, it is helpful to look at these in terms of the types of investments. Let's first take a look at stocks.

Stock Risks

"Company risk" is one of the most important stock risks. This is when a company fails to execute on its business model. This could be the result of poor management decisions, competition, or even major changes in the industry. Whatever the reasons, company risk can have a significant impact on a company's stock price, and it often takes time to earn back investor support.

Then there is "market risk." Even if a company does well, this may not necessarily matter. The reason is that the overall market—or industry—may be in a bear phase. When this happens, many stocks fall in value.

Next, there is a fairly hidden risk for stocks: "inflation." This is the general increase in the price level in an economy. So if an investment returns 5 percent but inflation is 7 percent, then the investor is actually sustaining a real negative return of 2 percent. Keep in mind that during the 1970s, investors sustained massive losses because of several bouts of double-digit inflation. In fact, inflation often causes instability in an economy, which could make it even more difficult for companies to operate.

Fixed-Income Risks

Fixed-income is another large asset class, which has its own set of investment risks. A major one is "interest-rate risk." Basically, an increase in interest rates will reduce the value of the existing debt investments, and vice versa. The reason is that there needs to be an adjustment to be competitive. Why would an investor purchase a security that yields 3 percent when he or she can buy another security—with identical features—that yields 4 percent? As a rule, the longer the "duration" of the bond—which is when the bond will be paid off—the more sensitivity there will be to interest-rate risk. True, it is possible to hedge against interest-rate risk. This is usually done by buying a short position with an interest-rate swap. However, this is mostly for sophisticated institutional investors.

Interest-rate risk will then lead to another risk: "reinvestment risk." If interest rates go lower, then the cash you receive from bond coupon payments will likely be reinvested in lower-yielding securities. The result is your overall return will be weighted down.

Fixed income securities also have "default risk." When a company issues a debt—such as a bond—it will need to get a "credit rating." This is an evaluation from a third party that the issuer can make the necessary payments. The main credit rating agencies include Standard & Poor's, Moody's, and Fitch Ratings. They will place a rating that varies from top-grade to junk status. Thus, the lower the rating, the higher the interest rate, so as to account for the higher risk level.

What if the bond is an obligation of a government? There is actually "sovereign risk," which is the probability of default. While such a thing is very rare, it can be devastating when it does happen. Even the threat of a sovereign default can result in a plunge in the values of debt securities. For example, this was the case in 2010 when the Greek government had troubles paying its debts. Other countries, like Argentina and Russia, have actually defaulted on their obligations.

Another factor for fixed income securities is "liquidity risk." This means that it is extremely difficult to sell a security. The reasons may include substantial levels of risk from investors or even a financial panic, such as what happened in 2008. When there is lots of liquidity risk, the values of the securities can fall significantly. It may be impossible to find a buyer, in which case the security has very little value.

Finally, there is "counterparty risk." This is mostly for institutional investments, such as credit default swaps (CDSs). Such instruments are an obligation between a buyer and a short seller. If one of the parties cannot come up with the capital to pay off the trade, then there can be a destabilization of the market. Again, this was the problem in the financial meltdown of 2008. During this time, AIG (American International Group) was responsible for many of these types of swaps. To preserve the financial system, the federal government ultimately had to bail out the company.

OPPORTUNITY COST, LEVERAGE, AND STUBBORNESS

We'll look at each of these topics, one at a time.

Opportunity Cost

When it comes to risk, investors often think about the potential loss on their investment. And this is certainly a major consideration. But risk has other consequences. One that is often overlooked is "opportunity cost." For example, in the meltdown of 2008, many hedge funds lost huge amounts of money. As a result, by the next year, they had little available capital to put back into the market. So they missed out on major market moves for 2009.

But this was not the case for investors like Warren Buffett. During the financial crisis, he was able to invest in top-notch companies like Goldman Sachs and GE—all at low valuations. In the end, these investments turned out to be big winners. The fact is that Buffett had a good amount of cash. True, cash typically generates a small return, if any. But it is good to have enough of it to capitalize on opportunities.

Leverage

Taking a conservative approach to risk often means avoiding leverage, or borrowing large amounts for a trade. While this will magnify returns, it does just the reverse in a down market. In some cases, an investor can be wiped out because of leverage.

Stubborness

Finally, some investors will simply not admit a mistake on a trade. Yet the market does not care. The stubbornness can result in significant losses. Great traders do not fall in love with their investments.

PORTFOLIO MANAGEMENT

For a short seller, it is easy to underestimate the overall risk level of a portfolio. Yet when it comes to short selling, there are potentially significant risks. Thus, it is important to periodically measure this on a portfolio-wide basis. To illustrate the importance of risk management, consider Table 16-1.

TABLE 16-1

The Importance of Risk Management

Portfolio Loss	Recovery Percentage
30%	42.9%
40%	66.7%
50%	100.0%
60%	150.0%
75%	300.0%

In other words, if your portfolio falls by 50 percent, you will need to get a staggering 100-percent return to get back to your original value. Needless to say, this can be extremely tough and may result in taking even more risks to try to compensate for the heavy loss.

Risk Management Strategies for Short Sellers

When it comes to short selling—and investing in general—there are some strategies to help with risk management. These often depend on the level of the investor's experience.

Take a beginner trader. When such a person begins short selling, it is a good idea to start slowly. This could mean taking one or two trades that represent a small part of the portfolio, say less than 2 percent. More importantly, the trader should monitor the trade frequently. If it goes up by 5 percent or so during a week, it is probably best to take the trade off and evaluate things.

Now, as for an experienced trader, he or she will start to evolve skills over time. This will not only involve good stock selection, but also trading rules. For such a trader, a portfolio may have 10 percent to 20 percent of short positions. And, if the trader is convinced the market is poised for a bear trend, the percentage may increase even more. But a trader will also attempt to minimize the impact of any position in the portfolio.

One approach is to use "the 2-percent rule," which means that no position may represent more than this percentage of the portfolio. Actually, this is often misunderstood. For example, suppose you have a portfolio of $100,000. An investor may think that the 2-percent rule means that *no initial position* may be more than $2,000. Well, this is incorrect. Instead, the 2-percent rule is about the *percentage of the risk* in the position. To continue with the example, let's say you short 100 shares of XYZ Corp. at $40 for a total of $4,000. But you also put a buy stop on the position for $45. This means that if the stock goes to $45 or higher, you will cover your position. This means your risk is about $5 per share or $500, which is only 0.5 percent of the portfolio. In other words, based on the 2-percent rule, you may short up to 400 shares.

There is also "the 6-percent rule." That is, if your loss for the month is 6 percent or more, then you should stop trading for at least another month. At the same time, it is probably a good idea to reevaluate all the positions in the portfolio. Are there some trades that no longer meet your criteria and should be unloaded?

TRADING RULES

A "trading rule" is a strategy for a particular short position. This involves several key factors. First, each trade needs an "investment thesis." This is the rationale for why the position will ultimately generate a profit. For many short sellers, this involves extensive fundamental analysis. For example, legendary short seller Jim Chanos uses the following methodology:

Fundamental Analysis from the Perspective of Jim Chanos

- The company has grown mostly because of a fad. However, there are signs that the momentum is sputtering and the company's sales and profits are likely to plunge.
- An industry has undergone a massive bubble because of excess debt. This happened with telecom in the late 1990s and real estate during 2007.
- Chanos is always alert to any accounting shenanigans. In fact, he was able to uncover notorious situations, such as with Enron, WorldCom, and Tyco.

- Is an industry going through a disruption because of technology? This can be devastating for existing operators. Just look at Blockbuster Video or Kodak.

True, there are many other short-selling strategies. For instance, a short seller may focus mostly on "chart patterns." Also, a short-sale trade opportunity may not have all of the factors in your methodology. But, this is OK. If several factors are evident, this should be enough to take a short position.

A short seller will then consider the trade's "weighting." Consider that if a trade turns out to be correct, the value of the position may represent a large part of the portfolio. This could add to the overall risk level. So, if you have a risk management policy stating that a short position gain may be no more than 2 percent of the overall short positions, then you should seriously consider paring back your position. This is a good discipline to have—and it also means you will be able to take some profits.

And all trades, especially those on the short side, will need to have some type of "exit." This is essentially when the investment thesis is no longer applicable. This could be because the company's sales are starting to increase or there is a major positive development (such as a new product launch). In this case, a trader will probably cover the short sale. On the other hand, you may have a short position that has lost money. This could be because you did not correctly analyze the company, and as a result, your investment thesis is faulty. Under this situation, the best approach is to cover the position.

No doubt, short-sale rules require lots of analysis, planning, and tracking. But successful short sellers will do this, which will help them generate strong returns with relatively lower risk.

STOP-LOSS ORDERS

A "stop-loss order" is a way for traders to control risk on a particular position. If a stock hits or moves past a certain price, an order will be sent to unwind the trade. As for short selling, this would technically be called a "buy stop-loss order." Of course, there are some limitations to stop-loss orders. First of all, a broker may not provide stop-loss orders for certain types of stocks, especially those on the Over-the-Counter (OTC) marketplace. Next, a broker may charge a higher fee for this service.

Despite all this, stop-loss orders are quite effective and experienced short sellers will often use them. Granted, it is possible to have a "mental" stop-loss, in which you will make the trade yourself. However, by placing a stop-loss order with your broker, you are allowing for more discipline in your trading, which can be critical when it comes to reducing the risk levels of short selling.

At what point should you place the stop-loss order? As discussed above, there is the 2-percent rule. In this case, you would place the stop-loss order at 2 percent above the current value of the initial short position.

Of course, this is a guideline. It could change from stock to stock. For example, a particular stock may have a high level of volatility, easily trading 1 percent to 2 percent per day. Thus, you may get a quick trigger on the stop-loss order. As a result, you may want to increase the spread to 5 percent or more. But if this is the case with several stocks, then it could be a sign that your portfolio is subject to large amounts of risk. In other words, you may want to be careful in taking on these kinds of positions.

Next, short sellers will often use "trailing stops." This means that as the position increases in value, you will adjust the stop. For example, suppose you short XYZ Corp. at $20 per share and place a stop at $22. Within a month, the stock falls to $18 and you will have a $2-per-share profit. You may then take the stop-loss order to $20 per share. But you would not adjust the stop upwards if the trade moves away from you. Instead, to allow for effective risk management, you should allow the stop to be triggered and get out of the position.

TAIL RISK

After the financial meltdown of 2008, many hedge funds continued to suffer from losses. Part of the reason was the difficulties in navigating the volatile markets. For example, traditional relationships between asset classes were not predictable. Also, institutional investors were increasingly pulling money out of funds, especially those with poor records.

For the most part, more investors wanted to find funds that would actually deal with low-probability risks. These funds are called "tail risk" funds and are based on the concept of the "black swan," from the best-selling book, *The Black Swan* by Nassim Nicholas Taleb. A black swan refers to the misconception that swans are white. But, interestingly enough, this is not the case. In fact, there are a decent number of black swans across the world. So, in reference to the stock market, a black-swan event is something that investors have overlooked because it is considered to be the worst-case scenario. And when do such events ever happen? Unfortunately, the history of the markets—especially in the past two decades—has experienced several black swans in the form of crashes, whether in the stock markets or in other areas (like real estate).

In terms of statistics—which is more comfortable for hedge fund investors—the black-swan concept is also known as a "fat tail." This is the outer part of the bell curve. But, since it is "fat," it is an indication that major market disruptions are something investors need to prepare for.

How does a fat-tail fund invest? There are several approaches. For example, a fund may time the market and go to heavy amounts of cash when there are growing bearish signals. There will also be a part of the portfolio short, such as with futures and options. So, when there is a plunge in the market, the leverage in these positions can result in substantial returns.

A key disadvantage of a tail-risk fund is the opportunity cost. You will most likely miss out on major rallies in the market. What's more, the returns will likely be negative because of the low returns on cash and the expenses of purchasing options and taking on short positions. So far, there are only a handful of tail-risk funds. However, if the volatility in the markets continues, this is likely to be a growth area in investing.

MACRO RISK FACTORS

When evaluating risk, many investors focus mainly on the fundamentals of a company or the industry dynamics. Yes, these are extremely important and are critical for making a successful trade. However, strong stock-picking is not enough. It is also important to look at "macro factors." These are the major forces in the world, such as monetary policy, inflation, unemployment, sovereign debt problems, and so on. In a global financial system, macro factors are becoming much more important and can have quick, major impacts on securities prices.

This even helps explain why asset classes have had higher correlation over the past few years. This means that they tend to go up or go down at the same time—and even roughly in the same amounts. The result is that it becomes extremely difficult to achieve diversification. After all, diversification is about lowering risk because some investments will increase while others decrease. So, by understanding macro factors, it becomes easier to avoid risks in the portfolio. At the same time, it may mean getting more short-sale candidates.

On its face, risk management approaches seem overwhelming. But if you focus on some key strategies, such as minimizing exposure to individual positions in the portfolio and using stop-losses, you will certainly be able to lower the risk levels. The most important thing is to have a discipline. After time, the risk management strategies will become second nature.

As for the remainder of the book, we look at various resources for short sellers as well as provide a helpful glossary.

Accounts Receivables: Sales of a company that customers have paid on credit. This is accounted as an asset. But short sellers will often look for sudden growth in accounts receivables as a red flag.

Advance-Decline Line: Shows the number of stocks up to those that are down. This is often a "contrarian indicator." That is, if the advance-decline line has increased substantially, the market may be at a top and poised for a fall.

Annual Report: Often a glossy publication, it shows the company's financials, as well as commentary on the future. A short seller will try to find clues of problems in the "Chairman's Letter," such as spotting words like "challenging."

Audit Report: Every year, a public company must get a third-party audit. The auditor will provide the results of this in a report. A short seller looks for any problems, such as a "qualified" report.

Bear Fund: A mutual fund that looks for troubled companies.

Bear Market: The general definition is when a market falls by at least 20 percent.

Bear Raid: This is when a group of short sellers aggressively target a company. Some experts believe that this happened to financial companies during the financial panic of 2007 to 2008.

Bond: Debt that a company issues, which usually matures in 10 to 20 years. In the meantime, the company will pay periodic interest payments.

The Borrow: The shares a short seller will borrow from a financial services' company to initiate a transaction.

Buy-In: This is when a short seller must buy shares and then use them to close out a short position.

Call Option: A contract that gives an investor the right to buy 100 shares of stock at a fixed price for a certain period of time. The investor makes money if the value of the underlying security increases.

Candlestick Charts: Developed several hundred years ago in Japan, this is a technique to chart the price and volume of stocks.

Capital Gain: The increase in the value of an investment.

Cash Account: The most basic brokerage account.

Cash Flow Statement: One of the required disclosures for a public company. A cash flow statement shows the inflows and out-flows of cash for operations, investments, and financings.

Chapter 7 Bankruptcy: A liquidation of a company's assets when it is unable to pay its debts. This usually causes shareholders to lose all the value in their holdings.

Chapter 11 Bankruptcy: A restructuring of a company's debts to allow it to continue its operations. While the company will likely survive, the shareholders will still probably lose all the value in their holdings.

Common Stock: This represents equity ownership in a company. The shareholder will have certain rights, such as voting and possibly receiving dividends. But in the event of a bankruptcy, he or she is last in line to receive any proceeds.

Convertible Bond: A debt of a company that matures in a period from several to 20 years. It will pay ongoing interest. However, there is a formula that allows an investor to exchange the bond for a certain number of shares in the company.

Correction: This is when the market has a temporary fall, which is anywhere from 5 percent to 10 percent.

Cost of Goods Sold (COGS): The direct costs for producing a company's products. The main components include inventory and salaries.

Counterparty Risk: The possibility that the other buyer or seller on the trade will not be able to honor the terms of the agreement. This is usually the case for complex derivatives, such as options, futures, and swaps.

Covering a Short: This is when a short seller closes out a short position and delivers shares to the financial firm that the original shares were borrowed from.

Current Assets: The assets that will turn to cash within a year. These include inventory and accounts receivables.

Days Sales Outstanding (DSO): This indicates how long it takes for a company to collect on its accounts receivables. If this grows, then there may be problems with the company.

Debit Balance: The loan from a financial services firm on a margin account.

Deflation: A general decline in the price level in the economy. This is often negative for stock prices, as seen during Japan in the 1990s and the United States in the 1930s.

Depreciation: The expense a company takes for purchasing equipment that lasts longer than one year. Some companies may try to understate this amount so as to show inflated profits.

Derivative: A contract between a buyer and a seller. Each is betting on the direction of a stock or other security. Common derivatives include options and futures.

Dividend: A payment to shareholders. This is often based on a percentage of the stock price and it is payable every quarter.

Earnings per Share (EPS): The earnings of a company divided by the number of shares outstanding. This is a highly followed metric on Wall Street. If a company fails to meet expectations on quarterly EPS, the stock price is likely to fall.

Efficient Market Hypothesis (EMH): The academic theory that says that it is nearly impossible for an investor to get stronger returns than the market averages over the long run. The main reason is that all public information is quickly incorporated into stock prices.

8-K: A regulatory filing for a company. An 8-K is for major developments, such as the departure of the auditor or a merger.

Exchange-Traded Fund (ETF): A pool of money invested in an index, like the S&P 500. An investor can buy or sell an ETF like a stock.

Exercise Price: The price an investor can purchase a stock on an option or sell it for a put option.

Federal Reserve Board (The Fed): The central bank in the United States. The Fed tries to allow for low inflation and steady growth through changing interest rates and the money supply.

Financing Activities: A category in the cash flow statement. It shows how a company is raising money, such as through stock sales or debt issues. It will also show share buybacks.

Float: The number of shares that are actually traded on an exchange. This can be much lower than a company's outstanding shares (which often have resale restrictions).

Footnotes: The explanations of a company's accounting policies. These are found in the 10-K and 10-Q.

Free Cash Flow: The operating cash flows minus the capital expenditures. Short sellers focus on this metric since it provides a better gauge of the company's cash-earning power.

Future: A contract that gives an investor the right to buy or sell an underlying asset, such as a commodity or an index. An investor will put up a small amount of the initial value of the contract, say 5 percent to 10 percent. This is done using a margin account.

Generally Accepted Accounting Principles (GAAP): The rules for public companies to comply when reporting their financials.

Going Concern: This is when an auditor reports that a company will have trouble paying its debt and staying in business. This is a major red flag.

Gross Profit: The difference between revenues and the costs of goods sold.

Guidance: A company's own estimate of its revenues and profits. This is usually for the next quarter and the full year.

Hedge: This is when an investor uses short selling or a derivative transaction to protect the downside of an investment.

Hedge Fund: This is a pool of assets from a variety of investors. Usually, they are institutions or wealthy persons. A hedge fund often has much latitude in terms of investment strategies, including short selling.

Hypothecation: A clause in a margin account that allows the financial services company to relend your securities to other investors.

Income Statement: A financial disclosure statement that shows a company's revenues, expenses, and profits or losses.

Initial Public Offering (IPO): This is when a company issues stock to the public for the first time.

Insider: An executive, director, or major shareholder in a company. They will have restrictions on the sale of their stock holdings.

In the Money: This is when the stock price is above the exercise price for a call option; the reverse is true for a put option.

Intrinsic Value: See *In the Money*.

Inventory: The raw materials, work-in-progress, and finished products that a company has yet to sell.

Inventory Turnover: The number of days it takes a company to sell its inventory.

Inverted ETF: An exchange-traded fund that increases in value when the index falls. So, if the index falls 1 percent, the inverted ETF will increase by 1 percent.

Inverted Yield Curve: A yield curve that is inverted rather than upward sloped. This occurs when the Fed is tightening monetary policy.

Investing Activities: A category in a cash flow statement. It shows the capital expenditures, such as for equipment, mergers, and software.

Liabilities: This is what a company owes. It includes accounts payables, notes, bonds, and unpaid taxes.

Limit Order: An order placed at a specific price when purchasing a stock. This is an attempt to get a better price.

Load: The commission an investor pays when purchasing a mutual fund.

The Locate: This is the process of borrowing shares from a financial services firm in order to initiate a short-sale transaction.

Lock-Up Agreement: A contract with executives, directors, and major shareholders to prohibit the selling of stock after an IPO. This typically lasts six months. The purpose is to prevent dumping of the shares.

Long-Short Fund: A hedge fund that uses a combination of long and short positions.

Margin Account: A brokerage account that allows the investor to borrow money or securities from a financial services firm. A margin account is necessary for short selling.

Marginable Stock: Stock that a financial services firm will allow loans against. If a stock is not marginable, then you will not be able to short it.

Market Breadth: See *Advance-Decline Line*.

Market-Neutral Portfolio: A portfolio that has roughly the same amount of long and short positions. The goal is to reduce the impact on the portfolio from the overall market.

Market Order: An order placed at the current market price when shorting a stock. While you will not get the best price, you will be guaranteed fast execution.

Minimum Maintenance Requirement: The minimum amount of assets required in a margin account. If the amount falls below this level, a broker will require the addition of cash to the margin account to raise the level to the minimum. If it is not paid, then the broker has the right to liquidate assets in the account to pay off the loan amount.

Moving Average: This shows the average price of a stock on a chart. This is often a 50-day or 200-day moving average. Investors will track these to get a sense of when a stock is ready for a move on the upside or downside.

Moving Average Convergence-Divergence (MACD): A common indicator for technical analysis. It is based on a 12-day and 26-day moving average.

Mutual Fund: A pool of assets that invest in certain strategies or indexes. Some mutual funds will engage in short selling, such as bear funds and long-short funds.

Naked Short Selling: This is when a person shorts a stock without borrowing the shares from a financial services firm. This is illegal in the United States, as well as in many other countries.

Off-Balance Sheet Liabilities: Debts that do not show up on a company's balance sheet. A short seller will try to identify these liabilities and get a sense of the overall risk of a company's financial position.

Operating Activities: A category in the cash flow statement. It shows the inflows and outflows of the day-to-day activities of a company.

Out of the Money: This is when the exercise price is higher for a call option than the current stock price; the reverse is true for a put option.

Preferred Stock: This represents equity in a company. A preferred stock has more advantages than common stock. For example, it will get priority with the payment of dividends.

Premium: The price of a call option or a put option. This is based on the time and intrinsic value of the option.

Prepaid Expenses: These are expenses paid for in advance, such as for advertising, supplies, rent, and insurance.

Price-Earnings Ratio: A company's stock price divided by the earnings per share (EPS). This provides a gauge of the valuation of a company's shares.

Private Investment in Public Equity (PIPE): An investment in a company's stock that usually involves institutions and hedge funds. These securities usually have more advantages than common stock.

Pro Forma Earnings: Earnings that are based on non-GAAP (Generally Accepted Accounting Principles). There are no standards for pro forma earnings and can be a way for companies to provide a misleading picture of the financials.

Prospectus: The document provided to investors in an initial public offering. It has the financials, as well as the business plan.

Proxy Statement: A disclosure that allows shareholders to vote on important matters, like the stock option plan and mergers. The document also discloses executive compensation levels.

Put Option: This allows an investor to sell 100 shares of a company at a fixed price for a certain period of time (typically three months). The value of a put option increases as the underlying shares fall in value.

Quarterly Report: Also known as the 10-Q, this shows the financial results for the first, second, and third quarters. The fourth quarter results are in the 10-K.

Related-Party Transaction: Transaction that a company or executive has that involves a conflict of interest. An example is when a CEO strikes a contract with a company that he or she has an equity interest in.

Repricing: This is when a company lowers the exercise price on the option grants for executives. The result is usually a charge to earnings.

Resistance: The price level where a stock price will encounter selling pressure. It is a key element in technical analysis.

Restatement: When a company must adjust its prior financial disclosures. This may be because of misrepresentation or even fraud.

Restricted Cash: Cash that a company does not have ready access to. The reason may be because it is meant for a certain customer.

Retained Earnings: The total earnings a company has generated since it has started.

Revenue: The money a company gets by selling products or services to customers. This is also known as the top line.

Revenue Recognition: The GAAP policies a company uses when it reports its revenues. The main differences involve the amount and timing of the revenues.

Reverse Split: This is when a company reduces the number of shares outstanding. This will increase the stock price. A reverse split is usually a large ratio, such as 1 to 10.

Risk Factors: Disclosures from a company that show the major risks for investors. These include things like litigation, problems with internal controls, and intense competition.

Sarbanes-Oxley Act: The wide-ranging securities law, passed by Congress in 2002, in response to abuses of Enron and WorldCom. This Act substantially increased the disclosure requirements for public companies, as well as the penalties for violations.

Securities Act of 1933: The federal law that regulates the disclosures companies must make when they issue securities to the public.

Securities Exchange Act of 1934: The federal law that regulates the trading of securities. It requires ongoing disclosure from companies and forbids fraudulent statements.

Securities and Exchange Commission (SEC): The federal agency that enforces the securities laws. The SEC can bring civil charges against a company for fraudulent disclosures.

Short Funds: Funds that focus mostly on short selling.

Short Interest: The number of shares shorted that have yet to be covered.

Short Selling: This is when an investor borrows shares from a financial services firm and then sells them on the open market. The goal is to buy back these shares at a lower price so as to generate a profit.

Shorting Against the Box: This is when the owner of shares shorts them to lock in the price. Any increase or decrease in the stock price will have no impact on the portfolio. However, this may mean paying taxes on capital gains.

Short Interest Ratio: This is the short interest divided by the average daily volume. This shows how many days it would take for short sellers to cover their positions. If this is a week or more, it could mean that there is a threat of a short squeeze.

Short Squeeze: This is when a stock price increases causing short sellers to cover their positions. This will create even more demand for the stock and could exaggerate the stock increase.

Short-Swing Rule: The rule that prohibits an insider from taking a profit on the company's stock when the holding period is less than six months.

Special Memorandum Account (SMA): An account where excess margin from a short position is deposited. An increase in the SMA enables the investor to short more of the stock.

Spin-Off: This is when a company distributes the shares of a division to the public.

Stochastic: A technical analysis indicator that ranges from 0 to 100. A stochastic shows overall extremes in stock moves.

Stop-Loss Order: An order for your broker to sell a stock when it reaches a certain price level.

Street Name: This is when the brokerage firm keeps the actual certificates. This makes it possible for the firm to lend shares to short sellers.

Strike Price: The price at which the owner of a *call option* can purchase 100 shares and the price at which the *put option* owner can sell 100 shares.

Stuffing the Channel: This is when a company ships large amounts of products to customers to temporarily increase sales. Short sellers see this as a red flag.

Support: In technical analysis, the price at when a stock will find more buyers.

Technical Analysis: This is the use of charts to look at trends in stock prices and volume.

10-K: A filing from a public company that shows the annual results. The full financials, as well as footnotes, are included in the 10-K.

10-Q: A quarterly filing that shows the financials for a public company.

Time Value: The value of an option that does not include the intrinsic value. The time value generally decreases as the option gets closer to expiration.

Treasury-Eurodollar Spread (TED Spread): The relationship between the London interbank offered rate (LIBOR) and the 90-day Treasury yield. When this increases, it is an indication that investors are getting more risk-averse.

Underwriter: The investment banking firm that manages a company's initial public offering (IPO).

Vendor Financing: A company that lends money to its customers to purchase goods and services. Short sellers view this as an aggressive policy and a red flag.

Visibility: This indicates the confidence a company has in its financial forecasts.

Volatility Index (VIX): This measures the daily change in implied volatility in the S&P 500. If there is a sudden increase in this indicator, it shows that investors are getting more risk-averse.

Yield Curve: A graph of the yields of short-term to long-term bonds (up to 30 years). In a normal economic environment, the graph will have an upward slope.

BOOKS FOR SHORT SELLERS

The Big Short by Michael Lewis (2010): Author of bestsellers including *Liar's Poker*, this book reads like a thriller. It shows how several short sellers were able to make a fortune from the subprime implosion.

Confidence Game by Christine S. Richard (2010): This book recounts the story of hedge fund manager Bill Ackman. Over six years, he took a massive short position in MBIA. The trade finally paid off when the markets tanked in 2008.

The CRB Commodity Yearbook: While the price tag is not cheap—coming to $150—it is the bible for commodities traders. Published most years since 1939, the *Yearbook* has extensive information on the supply/demand for all the key commodities. Much of the data goes back over 100 years.

Don't Blame the Shorts by Robert Sloan (2010): This is a look at the history of short selling, with the focus on the U.S. market.

Financial Fine Print: Uncovering a Company's True Value by Michelle Leder (2003): This book shows the fine details of interpreting financial statements. For example, the author shows how to read footnotes—in annual reports and other SEC filings—to find bad news.

Financial Shenanigans by Howard M. Schilit and Jeremy Perler: Now in its third edition (2010), this is the bible for detecting gimmicks and fraud in financial reports. The authors use many case studies, such as WorldCom, Enron, and Boston Chicken.

Fooling Some of the People All the Time by David Einhorn (2008): A high-profile hedge fund manager, Einhorn tells his story about how he put on a short-sale trade on Allied Capital.

Hedge Hunters by Katherine Burton (2007): The author interviews some of the top hedge fund operators like Michael Steinhardt, Lee Ainslie, and Julian Robertson. There is also an interview with famed short seller, Jim Chanos.

How to Make Money Selling Stocks Short by William O'Neil (2005): The author, who is the founder of *Investor's Business Daily*, looks at how to spot short-sale trades using technical analysis.

Risk Arbitrage by Guy P. Wyser-Pratte (2009): This is a comprehensive look at arbitrage strategies, with many examples using convertible bonds, rights, and spin-offs.

Sell and Sell Short by Dr. Alexander Elder (2008): The focus is on experienced investors. Elder looks at ways to manage risk and use sophisticated analysis of charts. He also covers options and futures.

Sell Short by Michael Shulman (2009): The author has his own newsletter, called the *ChangeWave Shorts*. He looks at how to analyze short opportunities and focuses mostly on using put options.

Short Selling by Frank J. Fabozzi (2004): This is a collection of academic papers. Some of the topics include portfolio management, valuation theories, and derivatives.

BEAR JOURNALISTS, BLOGGERS, AND NEWSLETTER WRITERS

While the financial media is large—with many top sites like the Yahoo! Finance and SeekingAlpha.com—there are still not many journalists who focus on this area. The same goes for newsletter writers. One reason is that short selling remains mysterious, even to veterans in the business. What's more, the topic generates lots of controversy and may even jeopardize advertising relationships. Does a company want to advertise in a magazine or Web site that has lots of short-sale picks? Despite all this, there are some top-notch commentators, blogs, and newsletters.

Back in 2003, Michelle Leder started http://www.footnoted .org. For most of her career, she has been an aficionado of SEC filings. So why not provide her insights in a blog? It was a smart move as footnoted.org has become a widely followed site. In fact, Morningstar bought the company in 2010. For a short seller, http://www.footnote.org is highly educational. You will get real-world examples of strong forensic accounting analysis.

Next, back in the dot-com days Dr. Paul Kedrosky started GrokSoup, which was the first hosted blogging site. He eventually sold the company for a tidy sum. Since then, Kedrosky has been an investor and commentator. He also has a widely followed blog called "Infectious Greed." In it, he takes a realistic view of the economy and different types of investment themes. His main areas of expertise include life sciences, semiconductors, media, and consumer technologies. His blog can be accessed at http://paul.kedrosky.com.

Another great resource can be found in Jonathan Laing, who has been a top writer for *Barron's* for more than 20 years. Laing has uncovered some of the biggest financial frauds of all time by heavily focusing his analysis on companies' financial statements. Over the years, Laing has not lost his touch. A prime example is a piece where he predicted the federal bailout of Fannie Mae. The article highlighted a fall in the bond prices of the company, massive losses for two consecutive quarters because of a fall in real estate prices and speculative investments (such as subprime loans), high amounts of leverage, and a spike in soft assets on the balance sheet.

Herb Greenberg, the senior stocks commentator on CNBC, is yet another reliable source to turn to. Before he joined CNBC, Greenberg spent 30 years as a financial journalist for TheStreet.com, the *Wall Street Journal*, and MarketWatch.com. His analysis is always in-depth and often has a bearish slant. It also helps that he talks to top investors and hedge fund managers.

INDEX